Issues and Insights
into
Church Planting
in
The Muslim World

Issues and Insights into Church Planting in The Muslim World

by
Ron George

Founder and International Director of
WIN International Associates

WIN Press
2000

Issues and Insights into Church Planting in The Muslim World—
Jointly published by Win Press, A divison of WIN International
Associates.

This book is dedicated to George Verwer, my mentor and friend for the
past 38 years and to all those foolish people who believe that they can
change the world.

Cover design: TONY SMITH

ISDN: 0-901012-04-2

Contents

Contents

Preface

One of the sights you see in the deserts of Morocco is the many cacti that dot the landscape and give protection to the village compound. These cacti bear a fruit that is sweet to eat but very difficult to pick. They are covered in tiny needle-sharp hairs that the unsuspecting tourist can find sticking into him if he is not careful. Muslim work is like this. Men and women won to Christ out of Islam are often lovely, lovely people but the process of reaching the heart is fraught with difficulties and dangers.

Today, following the collapse of communism, many missions and Christian workers are turning their attention to Muslim work as an alternative focus. In doing so they are rushing headlong into a brick wall of attitudes and issues that they do not understand. For example, the death of Bishop Haik in Iran could be seen as a consequence of an ignorant and insensitive approach by the West to the Muslim world. Few seem to realise that what once worked in a communist world does not necessarily now work in the Islamic world. Indeed the loss of face and honour gives rise to dangerous powerful forces that come from the resultant humiliation. In putting pressure on the Iranian authorities, in public, western agencies actually made the authorities there back down over the execution of Mehdi Dibaj, an Iranian Muslim convert. Haik was contacted by many of these agencies and thus was seen as an agent of Imperial powers. Of course, the Iranians had to 'level the score' and took out their revenge upon Bishop Haik. In the end they killed Mehdi anyway.

This book is an attempt to provide guidelines and insight to those seeking to make Christ known in the Islamic world, so that we might at least understand the context in which we are to operate. It attempts both to challenge others to play their part in the evangelisation of unreached peoples, like the Muslims, and to do so in an attitude of much love and patience. This might be in spite of the rejection and the hardness of heart that will be encountered.

Proverbs 27[5] says **"Better is open love than hidden love"**. We must also expose error and falsehood wherever we find it, in order to be faithful to our Muslim friends as well as loyal to the Lord who commissions us. This book therefore advocates love as both method and motive. I say this at the beginning, because at times the reader may find my comments seem harsh. This is not the intended stance just for harshness's sake, but because there is an inherently anti-Christian spirit to Islam (and thus against our Lord and mankind's good). In exposing this error we are being more faithful friends.

Counter-Attack

When the church and its witness start moving into the Muslim world, there is always a counter-attack by Satan. I would not want anyone who reads this book to become involved in Muslim work without realising that many who do become involved suffer physical, emotional or psychological damage.

How God Works

I believe it is mainly through suffering that Muslims are won to Christ. God uses his children to show the Muslim world what a real Christian is. In Isobel Kuhn's book 'In the Arena' she talks about the world sitting on the seats of an amphitheatre as observers, with the Christians being in the arena of life. It is as the testing goes on that God can turn to those sitting watching the church and can say, "This is what a Christian is". It is through suffering that hearts are touched.

This may be through family suffering like that of Mark Bliss, an AOG missionary to Iran. He was travelling with an Iranian Pastor (it was actually Bishop Haik), when they hit an unlit tractor late at night. His three children were killed along with Haik's child. As they lay on the ground broken and bleeding, local people ripped off watches and valuables from their bodies. Mark and his wife are still involved in Iranian work after 30 years of faithful service.

It could be suffering through friends or new converts. Some new Muslim converts have even gone through Baptism just so they can then leak the names of other inquirers to Muslim clerics. These people can then be dissuaded from attending meetings. In Shia Islam you are allowed to hide your faith if there is any danger to you personally. So, by extension, if Islam seems to be in danger from mission work then deception can be employed to bring it to nothing. After all it is only to the 'unclean' and 'the cursed' that you are actually telling these lies. Even here God is shaping you, moulding you into Christ's image.

It could be through suffering government pressure. Living in an oppressive society puts a toll on the visitor. In the Shah of Iran's time it was accepted that one in seven Iranians was in the employ of the secret police. This atmosphere of suspicion and distrust causes many to give up and move to more comfortable ministries. One missionary I know had a gun placed in his mouth by a Muslim police officer to put him in fear. To this day he lives in a western city afraid of living with the people to whom he seeks to witness. This drives you to God in prayer.

It could be through ill health, attacks against your supporters, or even your family back at home calling you to withdraw. The most subtle attack comes in the domain of one's mind. Questioning God's goodness, His ability to care for you and the lack of answers to prayer, that seemingly you struggle. A strong mind and will are essential to survive and yet the paradox is that when you are weak, then God can be made strong in you.

Remember, any successful advance into or against Satan and his kingdom will receive the most subtle and evil attempts to undermine that work. This may not come just from Muslims; it can come from within. Many pioneering missionaries have experienced the most bitter opposition, couched in religious terminology, from fellow Christians. This is often because of a developing clash of cultures, even within the missionary team. The more the missionary identifies with the people with whom he is working, the less like his western co-workers he becomes or stays. He moves away from western way of thinking and doing things whilst they remain fixed within their original home culture. They cannot understand or appreciate this shift and either remove him or shunt him aside in order to maintain a comfort zone for the way they act and live. The whole ministry could have needed to develop and grow in order to be more effective. They then risk losing a valuable worker because of their inability to accept change. An appreciation for and an ability to work with mavericks is essential. They are often 10 to 20 years ahead of their time and can save a mission from becoming irrelevant and fossilised. By removing them Satan scores a point.

Although our subject is about church planting in the Muslim world, I would warn you that all the books and all the lectures in the world will never prepare you for what you will face. Nevertheless the training received in working with your own local church is the best preparation for an overseas ministry, supplemented with specialist instruction, such as Islamics and communications.

I firmly believe that the next generation of Christian workers will need all the discipline and self control that an officer's course for the Royal Marine Commandos requires.

This book is not about technique or methodology per se but the realities of Christian work.

Ron George,
WIN International Associates,
Crowborough,
East Sussex,
England.

CHAPTER 1

A Layman's Look at Islam:
Lessons to Learn, Dangers to Avoid

In the last 30 years the Muslim world has featured prominently in most radio and television newscasts in some aspect or another. Before we try to interpret these signs of the times we must first build an historical picture to be able to view them in context.

A number of historical events have shaped the current day Muslim world, beginning with the great Indian mutiny of 1857. Britannia had ruled the waves for many years and the Sepoy led rebellion against British rule shook the growing empire. Previous to the British East India company's involvement with India it had been ruled by the great Muslim family of Moguls, but had become lazy, corrupt and effete. Most of the administration was farmed out to the East India company and Britain benefited from the arrangement. Then prophecies were given by Hindu Sadhus of the end of the rule by foreigners; Hindu and Muslim united together to overthrow the British involvement in India. This led to direct rule by Britain and the end of Muslim control of India. A so-called Christian nation came to dominate what had been sovereign Muslim territory. This shook the confidence of Muslims world-wide, since, they reasoned, if Islam were the truth and the only religion of God, Muslims must be the all-powerful ones.

Islam in Africa had grown slowly by trading across the Sahara desert into Northern Nigeria and the Gambia. However, this form of Islam was very much mixed with local African paganism. With the rise of Muslim rulers going to Mecca to do their Muslim duties, they began to realise just how far short they fell of practising and even understanding true Islam. This led to a number of wars by those rulers against both their own subjects and other tribes in an attempt to impose a more strictly orthodox form of Islam upon them. This again led to a greater European involvement in keeping the peace in the areas and subjugating Muslim rulers. These were the West African "Jihads" or holy wars of the 19th Century in Nigeria and Ghana. Again "Christian" Europe was giving Islam a bloody nose and the crusades were being relived.

The Ottoman Empire had been in existence for over 400 years. It had ruled parts of Europe, all of the Middle East and North Africa. As in India, it had grown lazy and Winston Churchill was to call it the "sick man of Europe". The First World War brought about a collapse of the Ottoman empire, as the European powers carved up the empire's lands for their own domination. North Africa and Syria went to France, Iraq and Egypt went to the British, thus securing the overland route to India, which was the jewel in the British Empire's crown. By 1922 all that was left became modern day Turkey, very much modelled upon the European "Christian" powers. The Sultanate was abolished and Islam was headless. Kemal Pasha Ataturk had actually been planning the reorganisation of the Turkish nation and stepped in to lead and guide what is today known as Turkey. He banned the Arabic script, thus turning Turks to a European alphabet, set up mixed schools, limited Islam to the mosque and modernised trade and industry. Some argue today that his reforms went too far, others argue that they did not go far enough. Thus the tensions in modern day Turkey.

This process of European and American domination of Islamic lands shocked many Muslims and angered others and continued into the 20th century. There was the invasion of Egypt by French and British forces in the early 50's to secure the Suez canal to prevent Nasser from nationalising it; the war between Bangladesh and Pakistan where Muslim fought Muslim; the Iran/Iraq war and the revolution in Iran. It continued with the Palestinian problem and the conflicts between Palestinians, Jordan and Israel. "How could such a small country as Israel withstand the combined might of the Islamic peoples?" they argued. The experiment with democracy in modern Muslim lands is seen to have failed on many fronts and this has led to the phenomenal rise of fundamentalism in Egypt, Algeria, Afghanistan, Iran and even the Philippines.

Today, conflicts with western governmental agencies are often overshadowed by internal discord between Muslims themselves.

There is a lack of identity, a crisis of belief, a yearning for stability and even a return among some to the Sharia law, the law that is seen to be the law given by God to Muhammad. It is supposed to be for all mankind and is beyond criticising. Also there has been a failure of the western democratic system, with its materialistic and amoral (at the least) philosophies, to meet the needs of Muslim communities. Others reject the 7th century Islamic vision of a feudal society and wish to incorporate more of a western-style 20th century form of Government and society, within an Islamic framework. This wish has led to yet further conflict and tension. Compounded upon these problems have been the devastating effects of natural disasters such as earthquakes in Bangladesh, famine in Sudan and population overspill in Pakistan, affecting both local and national populations. If Islam is true, why are they being punished in such a way? The response has been to conclude that it is because they have been bad Muslims and therefore need to return to the Islamic vision.

Few in the West can actually say they are unaware of the great family of Islam and its all-encompassing philosophy of life. Most are confused and perplexed as to what Islam is and many respond in a very natural and human way, in hatred and suspicion. These tumultuous events in the Muslim world can be interpreted from several view points.

We believe that God is answering the prayers and the blood of the saints that has been shed over the centuries. He is finally turning His attention, in a momentous way, to the Islamic world. This great, homogeneous, monolithic block of Islam is cracking under the pressure of the Holy Spirit, to expose Islam for what it is.

In 1962 I went to Morocco and found fewer than 10 believers in that great land. Today many thousands listen to the Christian radio programmes and small groups meet in secret in most areas. There is a growing church there and that phenomenon could be repeated over and over again throughout the Islamic world. There is no land where there are no believers in Jesus Christ. You could not find that 20 years ago. Today we are on the verge of a major growth in the church and it will largely depend on our ability to love, adapt and win the hearts of Muslim people who are looking for an alternative.

Many Muslims have come to live in the lands by which they were formerly ruled: North Africans have come to France; Indians, Bangladeshis and Pakistanis to England; Indonesians to Holland and so on. The great need for manpower that existed in post war Germany meant the recruitment of millions of Turks to Germany. *God was so concerned that Muslims hear the gospel that He brought the mission fields to the Churches.* Did we respond in the way that the Lord wanted us to? Some were converted and they have begun to establish Muslim convert churches in the West. Sadly many have been ignored by Christians for a variety of reasons including fear, suspicion and apathy.

Many Muslims living far from home are lonely and want to have friends. They are warm hearted, family orientated and away from their own environment. Just by smiling and going to visit them you can win great acceptance and build warm accepting friendships. In these close relationships they will often confide in you about their struggles and fears. This is a good time both to pray with them and also to give them, in private, a copy of the New Testament. Pray for them and ask God to reveal Himself to them as they read it. Other opportunities also come. At Easter, Christmas or even on Muslim festivals like the birthday of Muhammad, which changes from year to year, as well, of course, the Eid celebration you can give a gift of sweets and a Bible. This is most acceptable and often received with great joy. It is very different from giving the scriptures at a normal time, since that can be seen to be proselytisation. Be sensitive and you will win through.

Western education is also putting pressure on Islam. Islam has no tradition of critical analysis such as western education brings to information and ideas. Sad to say, many are turning to secularism after looking at the rather stunted and unreasonable answers that their leaders give to questions that the modern generation asks. Works by western Islamic scholars, many of them Christians, are being read and are profoundly altering the Muslim perception of truth. Students studying in the West have learnt to be critical about history, literature, physics, chemistry, engineering etc. and are now beginning to ask similar critical questions concerning the authenticity of the Qur'an, the validity of Muhammad and the supposed unity of the Muslim family unit. Books like 'The 23 Years' (Ali

Dhashti) are being written by Muslim scholars who have applied textual criticism to the Qur'an and Muslim sources only to find that they come up short of truth and veracity. This book actually claims that the first 13 years of Muhammad's life in Mecca were the only valid ones and that his 10 years in Medina were political and therefore non-spiritual. Consequently, once you have destroyed any part of the Qur'an, the whole house comes crumbling down. In the Times Higher Educational Supplement of September 15th 1995 Shabbir Akhtar wrote a most revealing article. Called an "Imam for all Seasons" he says that "Islam says nothing, it is Muslims who say many things". For a committed Muslim fundamentalist this is a major shift in his thinking.

Christianity has already gone through such academic attacks, but still it stands as a strong, viable force in the world today. It was born in persecution, has gone through the temptations of being popular and has breasted the wave of the enlightenment in the 17th century, when man and his intellect were elevated to a godlike position. These men believed that through reason man could find knowledge and happiness. Scepticism grew as an alternative to Christianity, history was seen as a straight path by man towards perfection. Recent events have shown that we are indeed not on a path to perfection.

Christianity has met these challenges and to this day still gives answers to man's questions because it is not fuelled by a set of philosophical precepts, but by a living person.

Islam has yet to face its "enlightenment" era (in fact, every indication is that it is approaching this stage) and is responding by demanding death for all those who dare to question its authority.

There are numerous new movements within the world of Islam that are questioning its very nature and trying to find a way to live in the 20th century. Iqbal in Pakistan tried to adapt and restate Islam in the light of his contact with Christianity. Other Indian Islamicists tried to adapt and modernise Islam. This was a response to their being exposed to the current scientific thought of that day and the fact that a Christian nation had replaced Islam as the ruler of India. Turabi in Sudan sees the nation breaking up unless Islam is adopted as the state religion and all others conform to it. Ali Dashti in Iran proposed that the verses of the Qur'an that came from the early period of Muhammad's life are the only true ones and that the others are not true. Many voices and visions in the modern era are trying to define what is Islam. The very world view and attitude of the Islamic faith does not allow for major change, growth or development to meet present day needs. Thus political turmoil, social deprivation, war and famine are the consequence. This is because the Islamic view is that man does not have to care for his environment; it is there for him to use as a gift from God to take and use, not to care for. Tribalism and national pride cause war and conflict and are governed by Islamic law. These problems are impacting the Muslim world as never before and when men's hearts fail them they become more open to seeking an alternative view of life and search for a fresh word from God.

Writers, painters, dramatists, film makers and journalists are all under threat because of their daring to question the interpretation that others have placed upon the Qur'an. Some have even been assassinated, especially in lands like Algeria, Iran, Egypt, Bangladesh and Malaysia. This struggle to accommodate critical thinking in Islam will result in an ever-increasing gap between the two and the overthrow of this western model. It seems that God's way is to give the people what they want and to send leanness to their soul. Iran has overthrown the western model of society and politics and is now in the process of trying to apply Islam and Islamic law to its citizens. In the process many are fleeing from the state it has created and so have become disillusioned with Islam. Thus thousands of Iranians have rejected Islam and many have turned to Christ as the only answer to the eternal problem of man: what to do with the sin that we find within us.

CHAPTER 2
Where is the Muslim World?

First of all let me paint a picture of how big and varied the Muslim world is. We are not talking about a small group of people - what we are talking about is 20 per cent of the entire global population, some 1,000,000,000 people. I believe that God is pointing us to a new way of reaching the Muslim world and I think we Christians must be aware of what God is doing now, in order to proceed effectively in church planting. The Islamic world stretches from Morocco in the west of North Africa through Algeria, Tunisia, Libya and Egypt. It takes in the whole of the Arabian peninsula, including Iraq, Syria, Jordan and Arabia and the Persian Gulf through the Persian block, Afghanistan down into India and Indonesia. To most westerners this Islamic block is huge and incomprehensible.

There are many ways of looking at the Muslim world. One way is to look at political nations created by western 19th century governments over the past 100 years. Another is to work within colonial structures such as French Africa or Dutch Indies. Another way is to look at the linguistic/cultural networks that have existed for over a 1000 years. We can see that these networks actually form great blocs of people bound by a common language and culture that goes beyond religious ties.

If I were to come to your lovely house and I knocked at the door and said "Could I tell you about my religion?" What would the average person say? Perhaps; "No, thank you; I am a Lutheran, a Baptist, an Anglican, I have my own religion" or possibly, "No, thank you; I have to cut the grass today." We get embarrassed talking about religion. What if instead somebody from your family comes and knocks at the door, you could say "Hello Uncle, I haven't seen you for such a long time, come in, come in! Where have you been? What have you been doing?" He comes in, you sit and drink coffee and he says "By the way I have become a Christian. Let me tell you how it happened ..."

What makes the difference? The difference is that there is relationship. Someone from his family is telling him about Christ. Muslims are very relational people and the anger and the resentment they feel is often because these relationships have been overturned and/or disregarded.

Paul, in 2 Timothy 2, challenges Timothy to train others in the faith as he also trained Timothy. To do this in a Muslim context must mean that we have to understand the mindset of the person we are training. That is, what they need to be trained in, what their particular cultural problems might be, their world view, their "besetting sins", as it were. It is no good applying an American course in discipleship to one coming from a completely different cultural background. We should just never make a single disciple. Paul says that we are to disciple others and he is an example of the way to do it. I think the day has come when we have got to begin to say "Where are the people that are related to these Muslim groups?" We need to establish firmly the concept of 'near neighbour' evangelism. That does not mean to say that others should not be involved but, if we want improved communication, we must consider this as a serious option in increasing the spread of the Gospel.

There are five identifiable Muslim blocs. First of all there is the **Arabic** bloc: there are 200 million Muslims in the Arab world, mainly within and through North Africa and the Arabian Peninsula. It includes Iraq, Syria, Jordan and the Palestinians in Israel and the occupied territories.

The Arabs come from the group of races known as "Semitic" people, after Shem, one of Noah's three sons. The Jews and Assyrians are also in the same group. To reach them there are the Egyptian, Lebanese and Palestinian churches that are now beginning to have a say in missionary activities. Some 400 Arab churches around the world are beginning to work together in order to form a network of co-operating bodies sending Arabs into missions. This is good news, considering the Arab tendency to work only under strong centralised leadership.

The second is the **Indo-Persian** bloc: over 200 million Indo-Persian Muslims with a similar language and a similar culture. Similar language and culture unite all of this bloc. This is one of the most varied and complex blocs of all. It includes the Kurds, the Persians, Dari speakers from Afghanistan, Wakhis from the Himalayas, Bakhtiaris of Iran, Tats and Ossetes with Urdu speaking peoples in both India and Pakistan and the Tajiks of Central Asia. A swath of approximately 260 millions from Diyarbakir in Turkey to Dacca in Bangladesh, depending where your boundaries of language and culture lie.

The third bloc is the **Turkish** which goes up into Central Asia and out to China. It starts in the former Yugoslavia, where there are many Turkish people, then to Bulgaria, through Turkey, Northern Iran and, following the golden highway of the silk route, across into Central Asia through Bokhara and Samarkand and then finally into China and Urumchi along the Gansu corridor of China. The Turks are a people that includes Azeris, Uzbeks, Kirgiz, Kazakhs, Uighurs, Turkmen and others. The population of this Turkic bloc is around 230 million people and their languages come from the Altaic family of languages, which takes its origins from the Altaic mountain region in Russia. There are probably not more than 2000 born again believers from this mass of humanity. Also coming from the same language group are the Koreans and Mongolians.

Then we have another 200 million in the fourth bloc, the **Malay** speaking people. The Malay language is spoken by the Indonesians, by the Filipino Muslims, and on all the islands of the south Pacific.

One of the most difficult and most frustrating areas to work in is that of the Malay bloc. Within Malaysia and Singapore there is a strong vibrant church from amongst the Chinese who live there. However, government policy makes it almost impossible for this local group of Christians to reach out without suffering a loss in living standards. It is illegal in Malaysia to witness to a Muslim Malay. There is a fine balance of power in the nation and if Malays were to convert out of the culture they could weaken the voting power of the Malay Muslims, who number about 54% of the Malay peninsula. Also the doctrine of racial harmony works against assuming that the other race (the Malays) do not have the Truth. Of course, this should not stop the Chinese Christians in Malaysia from fulfilling their God given task of evangelism, but materialism has robbed the churches here of the zeal that we often find amongst Arab churches, who also live under oppressive restrictions.

The fifth bloc is **Africa** south of the Sahara. It covers the great African Sahel, incorporates all the lands south of the Sahara desert and is made up largely of the black peoples, either Chadic or Nilotic by origin. God has a Christian group which is related to all of those African Muslims.

Now let us consider who could be a relative or better still a *near relative* to these Muslim peoples.

First of all, who are related to the Arabs? Where is there a large church that is related to the Arabs? The answer surprisingly is Latin America. South Americans are related to the Arabs. The Arabs ruled Spain for 800 years so the Spanish culture was largely formed in contact with Arab culture. This was then "exported" by the Spaniards when they conquered South America and took their culture with them. Through the Spanish the Arab culture was passed on to Latin America. The Latinos are in fact *near relatives* to the Arab world culturally. We are beginning to see South American Christians come and work in the Arab world very effectively. The Latin American attitude to women, family, culture and life is similar to that of the Arabs and so they can more easily fit in with the Arabs.

Not long ago I was teaching an anthropology class at Moody Bible Institute and was trying to explain the intricacies of Arab cultural lifestyles. To the 'Anglos' it was all rather strange, but to a Mexican in the class it was exactly the experience he had gone through to get to the USA. He had had to build connections with people, get introductions and borrow money in order to facilitate his acceptance in the American embassy in Mexico. So many times western Christians go to the Arab world but they cannot relate to the Arabs. They cannot think as an Arab thinks and they cannot understand the way of an Arab, so they get discouraged and go home or become ineffective. Of course there are also Arabs in Lebanon, Egypt and other lands. There are also a number of Palestinian Christians who are close to Arab Muslims in culture.

Where is there a large church that is related by language and culture to the Turk? It is the Koreans, because the Koreans speak an Altaic language. The Finns, the Hungarians and the Koreans all belong to this family of languages and so can relate to the Turks. A hundred years ago there were no Korean churches and yet today some twenty-five to thirty per cent of South Korea is Christian. I spent an Easter Sunday morning in one church which had seven thousand people in that single service. In all there were seven services just to be able to accommodate the whole congregation.

We find Shamanism common to both Korean and Turkic culture. Shamanism is the largest and most unorganised religion in the world. It is a world of spirits that exist in trees, rocks, hills, rivers and animals. It is found in Africa, Asia, Latin America and, of course, traditionally with the North American Indians. We might feel that it does not exist in the Anglo-Saxon world, but, of course, it does in the form of good luck charms, New Age teaching and superstitious practices. Our Korean brothers and sisters are therefore in a better position to understand and war against the spirits that bind this group to Islam. Language is a vehicle for transmitting a culture. The Korean culture has shamans in it, so also has the Turkish culture. Westerners have gone to Turkey but find the Shamanism present in Turkish Islam something they are not equipped to deal with. Many of the Koreans, however, have a relative (a grandmother or an aunt) who actually practises the black art. Koreans fit very beautifully with the Turkish culture. Here then is a *near relative* available for Kingdom work.

In the past 15 years God has been at work building a significant Persian church due to the fundamentalism that broke out in Iran. Many, for the first time, saw what Islam really was and turned away from it, looking for an alternative. God is also building his church among the Iranians in exile. As soon as they become Christians they are being taught to be a missionary as well. There is also a large church in North India coming from this Persian language group. There are similar churches in Pakistan. Mobilising the power and abilities of these believers into the Indo-Persian block is crucial to the success of effective evangelisation amongst these millions.

What about the Malays? Who are related to them? Workers with bold creative initiatives have been found amongst the *near relatives* of the Malays. These are the Filipinos, Indonesians, and the peoples of the Islands in the Pacific, such as Fiji, Samoa, Solomon Islands, Hawaii and the Maoris of New Zealand. God has indeed been bringing a missionary movement to birth amongst these believers, though not without cost. Three Filipino Christians were shot dead in Manila in 1994 witnessing to Muslims in the inner city. Other Christians have also been murdered in recent years.

It is possible to support Indonesian Bible school students in Palambang, Indonesia. Before they graduate they must plant a church in a Muslim area. They need as little as £20 per month to survive. The training they receive would not go down very well in the UK. They say to their Pastor, "I want to be a missionary". So the Pastor says "Right, come and live with me, cut the wood, wash the floor, work in the kitchen". For one year they learn to serve. Then they continue for two years in Bible School and then in the fourth year, before they can graduate, they have to go and plant a church among the Muslims. They go and live in a village, maybe 50 kilometres away from another church. They go from door to door and witness to all the Muslims in that village. They have to plant a church before they graduate. Why? These people have realised that you can have a piece of paper but never have the reality. So the church in Asia is beginning to become many times more effective than western missionaries. Theological education can actually damage your spiritual life and vision. Becoming a servant and learning to be obedient, they have found, is far more important.

Then, of course, there is a large and growing church in Africa. There are many Christians in Nigeria and Ghana and also down in South Africa as well. Little needs to be said of the African Church. Here we have a task force that has vision, training, zeal and experience of the Muslim peoples and languages. They are truly *near relatives* of the Muslim. However they need better training materials to offset the arguments being promoted by aggressive Muslims. They need funds to cover the costs of travel and living in other lands and they need material aid to express love to needy Muslim refugees and there are many refugees in the Islamic lands. Consequently I believe that we should make western money available to help these African churches. They can do the work more effectively. How much does it cost to send a western missionary to the field? Maybe £25,000 a year and yet for an African it is a hundredth of this figure.

From these examples we can see that the church in Asia and Africa is coming of age. They are learning new lessons and bringing their insights into missions for all to enjoy and participate in. Praise God for the variety and complexity in the body of Christ. This gives me hope that He will build His church in the Islamic world.

CHAPTER 3
Islamic Origins

Another purpose of this book is to try to simplify a very, very complex part of our world, bring understanding to the issues involved and suggest a way forward. The complexity is mind-boggling, with 1,000,000,000 people and some 3,500 different cultural groups spread throughout the world, hundreds of languages and many sects and cults within and outside of mainstream Islamic thought. It is possible to simplify many of these complex issues by looking at common themes in the regions and society as a whole.

Muhammad was born in 570 AD and died in 632 AD. During his lifetime he went from being a rejected reformer in Mecca to being acclaimed as a new prophet of God for the Arabs. During the last ten years of his life he subdued by one means or another the tribes of Arabia and took control of the city of Mecca as his centre of both religious worship and political power. Fundamentally Islam is a Jewish sect. I know our Muslim friends will not like my saying this, but any cursory glance at Islam will perceive its Jewishness. In the beginning Muhammad cast himself as a Jewish prophet and tried to be accepted by the Jews in Medina, a city he fled to when the Meccans rejected him. In Medina the Jews demanded proof of his prophethood and he says in the Qur'an that he has no evidence to offer other than the beautiful poetry of the Qur'an. This obviously was not enough for the Jews and they rejected his claims. This led to his turning away from Judaism and forming his own new religion based upon the facts he already had of Jewish religion and mixing them with pagan Arab practices.

Let us look at Romans chapter 10[1-3]. Change just one word in this block of verses and see the relevance. Change the word 'Israelite' to 'Islam' and we can see how the Islamic world fits perfectly with Paul's description of Israel. They have a zeal for God but are without knowledge. Because Muhammad was lacking both an open revelation from God and a Bible in his own language, he made mistakes. That is why there are contradictory statements in the Qur'an and the Bible.

Ali Dhashti, an Iranian senator, states that Muhammad's ministry was divided into two parts. For the first 13 years of his work he was like a prophet crying in the wilderness. He tried to persuade the people of Mecca that to bury baby girls alive, to oppress widows and to worship idols were wrong. To Khadija, his wife, he was very faithful and it seems they had a very loving relationship. However, in 622 AD. his whole world changed and collapsed around him. His wife died. His uncle, who had offered him protection against the merchants of Mecca, also died and the Meccans were able to persecute him openly. He fled 200 miles north to Medina where he became the governor of the city. Whilst in Mecca he had felt that God had been speaking to him. By using the technique of telling his followers that God had told him something, he made them listen.

The wars between the Byzantine Greeks and the Persians during Muhammad's lifetime had broken the trade route that went from Constantinople across Persia to China bringing silk to the Byzantines. This breaking of the trade route caused an alternative route to be born. This brought silk from China by sea to be unloaded in Yemen and brought by camel caravan up through the western Arabian peninsula through Mecca into Alexandria and Constantinople. With the coming of new trade through Mecca a number of things took place. First of all new wealth was created by trading and also by subsidiary services, such as hostels for the traders passing through. With the new wealth came an increase in population, but most important was the bringing of new ideas into the Arabian peninsula. Buddhists, Hindus, Christians, Jews were all involved in this trading venture.

This new day in Mecca's fortunes highlighted the fact that the old customs and deities were inadequate to deal with the new issues facing the traders in Mecca. A new system needed to be found to produce stability and answers to the traders' questions. Muhammad quite rightly rejected the multiplicity of gods, including some 360 gods in the Meccan temple, and chose between Christianity and Judaism to fire his spiritual thinking. His experience of Christianity in Arabia at that time was a sectarian one which believed in God the father, Mary the mother and Jesus the son (an interpretation of the Trinity promoting the idea of three gods), which he quite rightly rejected.

Muhammad therefore modelled his religious thinking in Mecca on Judaism, hence the Jewish practice of turning to Jerusalem to pray was incorporated into his practice. This became the focal point of his religious thinking at that time. However, when he arrived in Medina the Jews rejected his prophethood because of Deuteronomy chapter 18. They were challenged always to test prophets. Having failed the test, Muhammad therefore rejected Judaism as the source of inspiration and created his own religious thinking, based upon the fact that he had now learned from the Jews that Ishmael was the father of the Arabs. This myth continues to this day in many quarters. Consequently the direction of prayer or 'Qiblah' is now said to be Mecca, which is one of the first changes in Muhammad's thinking. This then introduces the doctrine of 'Abrogation' into Islam where one verse supersedes another within the same book. It is as if God changes His mind half-way through revealing His 'Book' to His messenger and comes up with a better idea. We can tabulate the origins of Muhammad's ideas on the next page.

Muhammad was a brilliant leader and strategist. He began to graft in all the pagan practices of Mecca into his early Jewish thinking. He claimed that Mecca was the temple built for the worship of the one God by Abraham and Ishmael. The Zamzam well, an old Arab holy spring of brackish water, now becomes the place where water was given, by the angel Gabriel, to Hagar and Ishmael. Mecca is seen as the centre of the earth. Therefore out of the hotchpotch of religious ideas in the Arabian peninsula at the time Muhammad picks and chooses different thoughts and welds them into one consistent Arabian whole, using Judaism and the Old Testament prophets as the basis of these ideas.

We therefore have Christian, Jewish, Hindu, Buddhist and Zoroastrian ideas along with the original pagan Arab culture all fused into one religious system called Islam. Up to the death of Muhammad there was no book called the Qur'an. It existed purely in the memories of his followers and was written down on bones, stones, leaves and bits of parchment. With Muhammad's death and

I. From Heathenism existing in Mecca or prevalent in other parts of Arabia.	a. Sabæanism:	**Astrological** superstitions e.g. that meteorites are cast at the devil. Oaths by the stars and planets (Surahs 50 & 53 etc). **Circumambulation** of Ka'ba - and the calendar. Allah, as name of supreme deity, used in old poems and worshipped by the Hanifs and others.
	b. Arabian Idolatry:	**Mecca,** centre of religious pilgrimage - The Black stone etc. Pilgrimage, in every detail: hair, dress, offerings, casting stones, sacrifice, running. Polygamy, slavery, easy divorce and social laws generally. Ceremonial cleanliness, forbidden foods, circumcision.
	c. Zoastrianism:	**Cosmogony** - the different stories of the earth; Bridge over hell, the Surat. Paradise - its character, the houris; pairikas of Avesta. Doctrine of Jinn and their various kinds. Exorcism of Jinn (Surahs 113 & 114).
	d. Buddhism:	The use of the rosary (see Hughes' 'Dictionary of Islam') 1. Words that represent Jewish ideas and are not Arabic but Hebrew.
II. From JUDAISM found in the Old Testament, but one especially - the Talmud, the source of Jewish ideas prevalent in Arabia just before Muhammad.	A. Ideas and Doctrines; (According to the division of Rabbi Geiger)	Taboot (ark); Torah (law); Eden; Gehennom; Rabbi, Ahbar (teachers); Sakinat = Shekinah; Taghoot - used hundreds of times in Koran. Furkan, etc.
	2. Doctrinal Views.	Unity of God. Resurrection. Seven hells and seven heavens. Final judgement, signs of last day. Gog and Magog etc.

		with water or with sand.
	3. Morals & ceremonial Laws.	Prayer; its time, posture, direction etc. Laws regarding impurity of body; washing. Laws regarding purification of women etc.
B. Stories and Legends (According to the division of Rabbi Geiger)	4. 	Views of life: Use of 'Inshallah'; age of discretion corresponds to Talmud. Adam, Cain, Enoch; the fabulous things in the Koran are identical with Talmud. Noah - the flood- Eber (HUD) - Isaac, Ishmael, Joseph. cf. Koran with Talmud. Moses - The fables related of him and Aaron are old Jewish tales. Jethro (Shuaib); Saul (Taloot); Goliath (Jiloot); and Solomon especially. cf. Talmud.
III. From CHRISTIANITY its corrupt form, as found in the apocryphal gospels, especially the 'Gospel of Barnabas'.		1. Reference for New Testament - Injil - (Zacharias, John, Gabriel) 2. Respect for religious teachers; the Qur'an references to priests and monks. 3. Jesus Christ - His names - Word of God, Spirit of God, etc - Puerile miracles - denial of crucifixion (Basilidians etc). 4. The Virgin - Her sinlessness - and the apostles - 'hawari' an Abyssinian word meaning 'pure ones'. 5. Wrong ideas of the Trinity. As held by Arabian heretical sects. 6. Christian legends, as of 'Seven Sleepers' 'Alexander of the horns' 'Lokman' (Aesop). 7. A fast month. Ramadan to imitate Lent. 8. Alms-giving as an essential part of true worship.

Chart of Islamic Origins. (Courtesy of Zwemer Inst.)

the expansion of Arabs out from the Arabian peninsula, some of them started fighting against each other because each group claimed to have the original Qur'an.

In Medina Muhammad's problems were different. He was no longer a prophet crying in the wilderness, but the governor of the city. He thus had status, power, weapons, men and a community to rule. Neither could he call on the counsel of his first wife, Khadija. One of his first acts was to begin to send assassins back to Mecca to eliminate those who mocked him by writing satirical poems about him. He attacked the Meccan camel caravans passing close to Medina during a month of peace. He was then able to offer any new follow-ers substantial wealth from the attacks on the caravans. His revela-tions now had to deal with political subjects and thus the Qur'an divides into two parts: the Meccan and Medinan surahs. The Meccan ones are basically religious chapters and the Medinan ones, written from 622 AD to 632 AD, when he died, are political chapters. Islam therefore is not a religion with a systematic theology but a political system in the name of God. How different from the life and teach-ings of the Lord Jesus!

It was at this point that Muhammad moved away from being a reformer of the Arabian peoples and took on all the characteristics of a sectarian leader. If we look at sects down through the centuries we find some common threads through all of them. Some of the most common features to be found are a preoccupation with sex; an attitude that all others are wrong and only he, the leader, has the truth; a desire for power; the death of all who oppose him (they are seen as enemies of God); the collection of wealth into the hands of the leader (Dr D. Seiver).

The wedding of culture, religion and politics was very much part of the medieval world, whether French, German, Spanish, Byzantine or Persian. This attitude was typical of the medieval period, prevailing at that time and common throughout Europe right up to the Enlightenment. This view was radically altered with the French Revolution and the end of the divine right of kings to rule. This attitude, however, has been set in articles of stone or "fossilised for ever" in Islam. In Islam politics are part and parcel of the very revelation of the Qur'an and the life of Muhammad. This causes a great many problems for the 20th century Muslim. No Muslim can be happy living under non-Muslim, secular, humanistic government and it is in the nature of Islam continually to work against any form of government that is not Islamic. We already have the formation of an Islamic parliament in Britain and, as Muslims grow in numbers and authority, they will insist on an Islamic form of government through which they can fulfil what they see as God's will for man.

Western political groups have their different ways of dealing with the Islamic presence, but the Christian must respond in the same way that Paul does in Romans chapter 10.

First of all his heart's desire was that they might be saved. Our hearts' desire for all peoples is that they might be saved. That is, saved from themselves, from sinful practices, saved from the bad aspects of their culture and environment and from satanic influence. This salvation is offered full and free because of the death and resurrection of Jesus Christ.

Secondly his methodology was prayer. Weak ineffectual prayer is one of the great curses of the modern church and where we have seen consistent fervent prayer mighty things have happened. The work of OM, YWAM etc. was all born out of nights and days of prayer. The world has yet to see what could be accomplished when men and women band together in commitment to one another and to fervent prayer for a task God puts before them; a deep loyalty would be established which nothing can tear apart and which claims the nations for Christ.

In the early years of Islam there were many clashes between Muslim armies, each claiming they had the true Qur'an. It was therefore decided to bring all these divergent groups together, with their parts of the text; they made one copy of the Qur'an and destroyed the bits and pieces, so that no more bickering could take place. There is therefore no textual criticism of either Qur'an or Hadiths in Islam and, of course, there is no original Qur'an either. By using the word 'original' Muslims mean that they believe the copies they have are like the original. There is also evidence that one of Muhammad's favourite wives, Aisha, whom he married when she was six years of age, had some parchments that were hidden under her bed. When they came to collate all these many pieces, some of hers were missing, since rats had eaten them. What was written on these parchments nobody knows and it is not possible to establish what the original Qur'an actually said. There is also evidence that some verses were removed. When Muhammad was speaking to Meccans, trying to get them to follow him, he allowed them to pray to Lat, Menat and Uzzat, three female goddesses, so long as they would follow him. His disciples objected to this, as he had already taught them that there was only one God, and he made the excuse that this was actually Satan putting verses into his mouth. These verses were subsequently removed from the Qur'an. There is no way of knowing what other verses were also removed from the Qur'an during his lifetime. Of course, our Muslim friends would fervently deny this, since to accept it would be to admit a corruption of the Qur'an and subsequently they would have to follow the teachings of the Bible. This they could never do. Rick Bailey, a modern researcher, has actually identified 88 different mistakes in the Qur'an.

CHAPTER 4
Why is it so Hard to Win Muslims?

There are many chains that bind a Muslim to Islam. Here are eight key elements, although others do exist.

1) The first chain that binds a Muslim to Islam is Islamic law, **'The Sharia Law'**. The word 'Sharia' actually means or indicates a pathway leading through the wilderness to a place of refreshment, like an oasis. The pathway is narrow, therefore the law is seen to be a restrictive force upon a Muslim's behaviour. This restriction is to prevent him from doing wrong or making mistakes and should lead to a refreshment of his soul. In actual fact it is a system of rules and regulations that give him his identity. It tells him what he can eat, how he is to speak, what happens at birth, life, burial, how he is to marry, how he is to divorce etc. For example, if a man is eating a water melon and has seeds in his mouth, how does he spit them on to the ground? Does he put them in his hand first and then tip them on the ground or does he spit them directly? The law should guide him on this. It is seen to cover every conceivable area of human life and activity and is to be followed absolutely, since it is a law supposed to have been given by God. Islam is therefore seen as a revelation of the will of God, whereas Christianity is a revelation of God himself. This is not unlike Jewish law, which has much to say about keeping the Sabbath. I remember a dear friend who worked his way through college. He would be employed by Jews in the Chicago area to light their fires and even turn the house lights on and off in order not to break the Sabbath teaching about not working on that holy day. He, not being a Jew, could be used to do things that they themselves would not do.

These fundamentals are very important to understand, because they will help us in our own spiritual journey. Neither in the Bible nor in the Qur'an is smoking of cigarettes allowed or disallowed.

It is just not mentioned. Therefore Muslims have the freedom to smoke cigarettes but not to drink wine, as wine is prohibited.

The Bible gives us a revelation of the character of God who is holy; therefore anything we do that is not holy or 'healthy' is wrong. It is against the nature and character of God. Smoking is therefore not usually seen as being a healthy habit for Christians. The chain-breaker for this is 1 Corinthians 9, where Paul says he is under the law of Christ, which, of course, is the law of love. 1 Corinthians 13, Perfect love casts out fear but the law brings fear. Chain breakers are great metal shears that are used to cut men free from their shackles. In this case we mean that Christ sets us free from such legalistic law-keeping by showing us that the law of Love actually fulfils the law's demands. For example, if I love someone, then I will not want to slander them, steal from them or do anything that harms them. Love therefore gives us a higher means of keeping the demands of the law and at the same time sets us free from a soul-destroying bondage.

2) The **Umma** or Mother community that a Muslim belongs to, if there is any sin, can ostracise him; the community regulates itself. We westerners are individualists and right from birth are taught to think for ourselves, make our own decisions, choose our own career and even choose our own wives and husbands. This is a strange concept, since a Muslim finds his identity in community and is always part of a group or an extended family in Islam. The purpose of this is to help the family survive in difficult times. My own landlord in Teheran had three children. One he put into the French Catholic school, another he put into the American Presbyterian school and the third he put into the Mosque school; thus he had a foot in three different camps. If there was a problem with the Europeans, he could go to the French school. If there was a problem with the Americans, then he could go the Presbyterian school and if there was an Islamic revolution, then he could also go to the Mosque school and claim that he was a faithful Muslim. There is therefore a plasticity to family politics that exists to enable family survival as opposed to being in place as consistent guiding element.

When a Muslim becomes a Christian, he is often cast out of this community. This is one of the most ancient and severe of sanctions that a community can impose on the convert. The Hindus do the same thing and Jews will hold a funeral service for one who becomes a Christian or changes faith. Therefore, when a man is considering the claims of Christ, he also must consider the effect it will have on his family, his village or tribe and ultimately his country. Few in the West would face such depths of ostracism. A Muslim has to consider these wider issues when he examines the claims of Jesus Christ.

Since a Muslim's perception of the 'Umma' is one of close community, they are very critical of the western lack of an ideal of community such as they have. Its attitude towards the old and women and an all-pervasive godlessness is rejected by them and is often seen as a result of having a wrong view of God. They perceive all western societies, and their constituent elements, as being Christian, including the excesses of Hollywood, blue films from Denmark and, of course, the curse of AIDS. One Islamic apologist has been circulating videos against the Bible and Jesus Christ and adding to it the testimony of Jimmy Swaggart when he confessed on TV to adultery. What we have to understand is that we are Christians not because we are perfect, although we aim for high standards, but because we are forgiven. Belonging to a community does not make me a Christian, Muslim or Jew but in their view it does and should. I am a Christian because I am forgiven, not because I was born in the UK or am a member of a Christian community. The element of being forgiven is not present in Islam in the same definition as it is in the Bible. Muslims find it quite repulsive to think that we believe an innocent man died in our place or in fact that a man could take our place before God. This is quite true, except for the fact that Jesus was God and so can do anything that He chooses to do. Thus the character of Christ is intimately bound up in His works. I believe, therefore, we have to disciple a Muslim as to the cost of following Christ and the implications of being a Christian long before he actually becomes a Christian. They should understand clearly what will happen in following Christ.

The biblical equivalent of the Umma is in John chapter 17, where Jesus prayed for his disciples to be one "....so that they may be one as we are one" John 17 v 11. The church is God's divinely blessed community. It is made up of people who have been born of the Spirit of God in a supernatural way; it is unique. The church should be an alternative society, providing comfort, healing of damaged lives and support in times of distress. Too often it has been replaced by a culturally bound reduction to a tradition that misses out these higher purposes. Unfortunately there has been a treacherous selling out of the gospel by reducing Christianity to a Sunday morning and afternoon service, missing the real thrust and purpose of the church.

Few churches reflect the revolutionary teachings of Christ and His call to evangelise the world. Often when the church should be the training place for those called and gifted for missions, it fails to see beyond its own needs. Therefore major missionary movements have arisen to take on that role. As water will seep out and find its own level, so also the spirit of God will always overflow the blockage and find a way to reach out to the lost. The Christian church was originally intended to be a community of God's people who committed themselves to one another and to the moral and spiritual integrity and improvement of one another's lives, every day of the week. Muslim converts must therefore be incorporated into a living body of committed Christians rather than encouraged just to attend church once a week. Too many times Muslims are converted and then fall away again, because they cannot find a warm and accepting community within which to grow and find meaning.

The Muslim Umma or community is seen to be one, therefore a Muslim should feel at home travelling anywhere in the Islamic world. In actual practice this does not work and a great deal of animosity, conflict, racism, and political persecution takes place between Muslim and Muslim, indicating once again the very human basis and experience of the Islamic institution. Many Muslims have fled to Europe to escape the rigours of Islam. During a seminar at London University, President Bhutto's aide called for a re-think with regard to Islam. He stated that nowhere in the Islamic world was there one square inch where there is freedom of expression, a place where he could go to speak his mind and express his opinions without the fear of death, imprisonment or persecution. Many flee to Europe to find the freedom that is denied them in their own lands. They continue to cling to Islam because, they say, it is not true Islam that is being imposed in that land that they have fled

from. Instead of turning to the church and the gospel they fall into
secular thinking and, in the past, into communistic visions of an
ideal society or into the arms of extreme fundamentalism which
seeks to return to this idealised image of what Islam is.

   3) **Tawhid**, the Oneness of God. It may seem strange for us to
identify the oneness of God as being a negative influence on Muslims, but maybe it will help if we actually specify what the nature
of God is like in Islam. There is an Arab poem which says that
'anything your mind arrives at, I tell you flat, God is not that'. God
is always transcendent, above anything that your mind can arrive at.
This is so that God can never be reduced to definable terms. He is
more like an extraterrestrial black hole. He is all-powerful, but you
cannot define Him. Muslims interpret the term 'Son of God' as
meaning that God took a wife called Mary and had sexual intercourse with her to produce Jesus: their understanding of the Christian Trinity. They are therefore very anxious to preserve the oneness
of God. He has no partners or equals. Whereas, instead of being a
unit as in Islam, God is a unity in Christianity in three persons. I
think we need to have a little more compassion and understanding
for our Muslim friends' problem, as I doubt that many Christians
can actually explain the Trinity. This is to be expected because, if
we were able logically to explain everything about God, we should
not need revelation. The very reason people claim to have revelation is that the greatness of God is so mysterious. The Bible is a
revelation of what the character of God is like and still 'we see
through a glass darkly' (1 Corinthians 13). One day, when we get
to be with Him in glory, we shall understand more. It is therefore
not very helpful to argue with Muslims concerning the Trinity or
Jesus being the Son of God. We should concentrate more on Jesus
being the 'Word of God' which is something they understand or at
least accept. John 1 tells us that in the beginning was the Word, and
the Word was with God, and the Word was God. We can point to
the fact that the Qur'an tells us that Jesus is the Word of God. John,
of course, is quoting directly from Genesis chapter 1, linking the
Word of God (Jesus) to the same Word that created the universe.
This puts a new dimension on the nature of Christ, who then became flesh and dwelt among us. It is interesting that the majority of
Muslims who do become followers of Christ actually turn to Him

because He appears to them in a dream. Here we see the Word being made real to them in a way that they accept and understand. Once a dream has occurred, the usual Muslim problems with the Trinity and other Christian concepts seem to melt away. Indeed it is the word becoming flesh.

4) **Insan al Kamil.** This is an Arabic term meaning the most perfect man and relates to a title that is given to Muhammad. In the Qur'an Muhammad claims over and over again that he has neither prophecy nor miracles to substantiate what he claims to be - a prophet come from God (Surah, or chapter, 13, named 'Thunder', v 47). Later, after his death, Muslims began to invent stories called 'Hadith', which elevated Muhammad from the position of lowly prophet crying in the wilderness to that of being almost the divine light that comes from God. In fact, some state that, if it had not been for Muhammad, God would not have created the universe. He is given the position of a saviour by the statement in the Hadith that he stands at the right hand of God and intercedes on behalf of Muslims, so that they are able to enter heaven. He is said in the Hadith to do miraculous things, such as healing and feeding multitudes of people.

There are some 600,000 Hadith; these were collected by various Muslim theologians some 200 years after the death of Muhammad. Many of these Hadith were actually rules and regulations which existed in Jewish and Christian cities such as Basra, Damascus and Alexandria and were incorporated into Islam and given a Muslim story to justify their being adopted. Most of the Hadith are quite difficult to accept as being true (See Schacht chapter 1, part 1 - 'Origins of Muhammadan Jurisprudence.'). For example, one day Muhammad was walking along the road with two friends and they came across a grave from which there were screams coming. Asked by his friends what was happening, Muhammad said that the man in the grave had wetted his trousers whilst praying and therefore the angels were punishing him. He then plucked some leaves off a tree, put them on the grave and said that when the leaves dried they would stop punishing the man (Al Bukhari). Another one tells of Muhammad in the desert wanting to relieve himself but lacking privacy. The trees and stones therefore gathered themselves around him in a circle to provide shelter (Al Bukhari).

There is also clear instruction on how Muhammad made love to his wives during their menstrual cycle. The 'gospel' of Islam is therefore not in the Qur'an but in the Hadith and relates to stories, true or false, about Muhammad, which often contradict Qur'anic teaching. Muslims rely very heavily upon them to give them a picture of the power, majesty and wonder of this man who himself claimed to be just a simple human being. The biblical equivalent or chain breaker for this is the fact that we have a greater than Solomon in our midst and that Jesus rose from the dead (Colossians).

5) **Tasawwuf,** Mysticism is very strong in Islam. It often equates to folk religion (which all religions must struggle with). There are a number of schools of mystical thought that give their disciples certain exercises to follow in order to obtain and experience deity. The experience rather than objective truth therefore becomes more important and it is very difficult to discuss or argue with the person who has actually had such an experience. One of the most common forms of Islamic mysticism is where a verse of their scripture is repeated over and over again in either a sitting or a dancing position - a mantra in Hindu terms. It is not unlike some fringe Christian groups that continually repeat the name of 'Jesus', work themselves into a frenzy and have a so-called mystical experience. However, it would be quite possible to do the same thing with the words 'Coca Cola' and receive the same kind of experience! It is the rhythmic repetition of words and the movements of the body that produce a trance-like state. In the Bektashi order in Turkey disciples actually spin around with the right hand pointing to the heavens and the left hand pointing to the earth to the accompaniment of beating drums. After one or two hours of spinning around on the same spot I think anybody would have an 'experience'. We shall discuss more about 'experiences' later in the book. We are told that we are not to follow cunningly devised fables (2 Peter 1[16]) and thus to follow the writings and deranged teachings of men who seek to gain control over us or to lead us into deviant experiences.

6) The next chain that binds the Muslim to Islam is known in Urdu as '**Sharm**' and in Arabic as '**Khajal**' and equates to our word 'shame'. Of course, all societies use shame as a control mechanism against those who would be different. In the Muslim world this shame factor is extremely strong. When a man is considering

conversion, his family will plead with him not to deny the milk that
his mother gave him in babyhood. His mother going to the market
will be laughed at as being the woman whose son became a Christian; a man in a factory will be mocked as being the man whose son
became a Christian and therefore the whole family will turn against
that person and put pressure on by pleading with him to come back
to the Muslim family. This then, when it does not take effect, turns
to death threats, which are often carried out. I think few Christians
realise that Jesus is our shame, that he hung naked on the cross,
despised and rejected by even his closest friends (Isaiah 53). Those
wishing to follow Christ will also go through this experience: rejection and humiliation. One dear friend who worked on my team in
Iran in 1965 was eventually poisoned by his own mother because
he had become a Christian. Philippians 2^{5-8} points out how Jesus
humbled himself and became obedient unto the cross.

> "Your attitude should be the same as that of Christ Jesus: who, being
> in very nature God, did not consider equality with God something to
> be grasped, but made himself nothing, taking the very nature of a
> servant, being made in human likeness. And being found in appear-
> ance as a man, he humbled himself and became obedient to death -
> even death on a cross!"

If they did this to Him, surely his followers will also suffer
shame, since the disciple is not greater than his master.

7) Nowhere in the Qur'an or Islam is **Shaitan** or **Satan** defeated. Few of us realise how important the defeat of Satan by
Christ really is. In Islam he is an object, along with his demons, to
be feared and placated in some kind of magical way. Good luck
charms and curses etc. are common to the Muslim. Not long ago I
was sitting in a restaurant in Kansas City, America, talking to a
thoroughly westernised Tunisian Muslim. There was no way of
getting through to him until I suddenly hit upon the thought of
sharing something with him: that there are often forces that we do
not see, that they are all around us and that we need to be careful.
He then pulled out a gold chain with the hand of Fatima and the eye
of God on it and told me a very interesting story. He had been
involved in a car accident and had phoned his father back in Tunisia, from a hospital in the United States. On telling his father that
he'd had an accident the father was quite at ease. He said "Yes, I

know that you were involved with a red car which you rolled over on the freeway. I went to a woman in our village who saw it happening in her mind and told me that you would be all right". Since that day he has carried a good luck charm to keep away the evil spirits.

The spiritual dimension is one that western Christians often neglect or don't understand. We must come to terms with this feature of Christian witness. Spirits are also blamed for making Muslims do wrong. There is no doctrine of original sin in Islam, only that man is weak. He therefore needs to be strengthened against these spirits by keeping the law, which is seen to be a hedge around him (as communism was to the Russians). If the Islamic law is practised, it becomes a means of perfecting the individual; he will not sin. The purpose of these spirits is to make him sin so that God can have an excuse for sending him to hell.

There has been a greater awareness in many churches in recent times concerning the nature of spiritual warfare. This has partly been brought about through greater emphasis upon the work of the Holy Spirit, but also partly due to the break-up of long held Christian values and the decline of our civilisation in the last few years. Of course there has been some extremism in all this, but it has been in the area of trial and test, leading to a growing practical knowledge and experience of the subject. There has probably never been a time such as now when there has been such an emphasis upon prayer and waging warfare for the gospel's sake. This must lead to good things.

7) Finally we must not neglect the fact that **Muslims fear God**. He is an awesome figure, one to be feared and obeyed without question. This fear causes a great struggle in their heart and mind when considering leaving Islam and becoming a follower of Jesus Christ. The only equivalent I can think of is the kind of fear that has gripped people who have lived within a religious sect. They have lived with the teaching all their lives that they, and they only, hold the truth. On leaving the sect they invite the wrath of God on them and their families. Throughout Islam man is caught in a web of fear: fear of man, fear of community, fear of family and fear of God, fear of loss of face and social ostracism. The Christian can offer a God who is a father figure, one who knows and cares for us in a myriad

of ways. His patience and love wait for us to come to him and also to respond out of love and not a sense of duty and law. This view of God, once known, becomes a powerful attraction to Muslim friends, but we must wait for them to come to recognise and understand this new concept of God.

Sources of Authority

When a Christian wants to know how he should behave or what he should believe, he usually turns to the Bible, the Christian community and/or church history as a source of guidance. The Muslim has many sources of guidance and authority but there are four in particular: the Qur'an, the many Hadith, the Ijma and Qiyas.

The Qur'an

Obviously the Qur'an is a very important source for information about the will of God, but in fact it has only six laws within it that identify punishable sins: highway robbery, blasphemy, alcohol, apostasy, adultery and false accusation against women. These all arose out of the experience of Muhammad and his family. He gave specific instructions regarding the punishment due to those who commit such offences. For example, his wife Aisha was accused of adultery after having stayed out at night in the desert with another man. On her arrival back in the camp others demanded her punishment, since adultery was assumed in that society. A revelation came to him that she was innocent and that those who falsely accuse women of adultery should be punished themselves.

The fact that the Qur'an does not present an all-round set of laws for the conquests to come indicates that it in fact was never intended to be used to be a guidance for mankind.

When the Muslims broke out of the Arabian peninsula and captured cities like Damascus and Basra, they hugely lacked the necessary guidance required to rule a new civilisation. The Qur'an is primarily a book of prayers and is about the size of the New Testament. As we have already stated, it falls into two sections: religious from the time that Muhammad was in Mecca and political from his time in Medina. It is simply not adequate for guidance in all matters. The New Testament is often looked down upon because it does not offer a model of the ideal society, a model accurately spelled out. The objective of the New, as well as of the Old, Testament is actually to present a clear understanding of the character of God. I was once challenged by a Muslim friend on this point that my book had no instructions as to how to run a nation. I felt defeated until I realised that it never was intended to portray a perfect model for all societies and cultures for all time. It gives a detailed portrayal of God's nature and therefore, once I know what He is like, I can seek to be like Him in any clime or time.

The Hadith

After Muhammad's death there grew up a whole series of stories that were invented by Muslims in order to justify the incorporation of existing rules and regulations that they found in the Persian, Greek and Egyptian empires that they had conquered. There were so many of these stories or Hadith that by 850 AD there grew up a whole collection of sayings that said that from then on there were no more Hadith to be invented. These were eventually collected by people like Abu Muslim and Termidhi into great volumes. They travelled the Islamic world, talking to people who had known people, who were supposed to have heard Muhammad say this or that. As the Qur'an does not come under any kind of critical analysis, neither do these Hadith. One is allowed only to examine the characters of the people that were supposed to have passed these stories down verbally to the time they were written in the middle of the 9th century. For any Muslim, especially those educated in western institutions, they are a source of great embarrassment. Even the Hadith were not in themselves enough to help control the huge empire which stretched from Spain to China. Therefore out of one of the Hadith there developed a new concept. At one time I spoke in a graduate meeting at Cambridge University. Many intelligent Muslims were there and so I quoted some of the more outlandish Hadith to them from the books I had bought in a mosque. This effectively silenced their arguments and we were then able to deal with real human issues regarding life and God.

Ijma

Muhammad is supposed to have said "My people will never agree upon error". This is seen to mean that if all Muslims agree on something it therefore must be true. The problem today, of course, is that you'll never get a thousand million Muslims to agree on anything. Thus it has come to mean in practice that there is an enlightened group of teachers, or 'Ulema', who are well versed in Islamic law and can give guidance to the community on issues relating to the modern practice of Islam. Therefore this became an authority for the Muslim clergy or 'Ulema' as it is called, as a lawmaking body. There are fundamentally five schools of law that have survived the centuries. The Shafi are traders and have taken their school of law to places like Indonesia and Malaysia. The Hanbali are more strict and orthodox and exist in places like Saudi Arabia and Libya. The Hanafi are more common, since this is a very pragmatic and practical source of Islamic interpretation of the law, and they exist in Pakistan, India and Turkey. The Maliki are from North Africa and are a very small group. The other is the Shia, who exist in Iran and other parts of the world but constitute less than 10% of the Muslim whole. Finally a more modern form is called Tatbiq, the combination of parts of any of the previous schools into a new system which suits the needs of the individual, found particularly in Egypt.

These schools or "Madhabs" are often mixed with modern European law due to the influence of European nations in the history of these nations. Thus a process of re-establishing true Islamic law is taking place but causing much conflict and pressure in the process.

Qiyas

This is the old Greek philosophical approach to life using analogy. If an issue arises in the Muslim community that needs an answer and there are no clear cut directives on what to do, it is allowed to make an analogy based upon either a verse in the Qur'an or one from the Hadith. For example, when Bourgiba of Tunisia wanted to introduce the concept of one man one wife into his country, he was wise enough to look to the Qur'anic source and actually to re-interpret the scriptures in the light of modern needs. The Qur'an seems to allow a man to have many wives, but in terms of insurance and pensions this is extremely expensive in today's world. He then looked at the text and saw that it said that it was permitted if the man could treat all the wives equally and, of course, he cannot. This, Bourgiba (or his advisors) said, actually meant that a man was allowed only one wife. Thus the law was changed on the basis of analogy.

When I first became a Christian, I was told never to put rubber stickers on the soles of my leather shoes because the Bible was against it. What the teacher meant was that the Bible had certain teachings about mixing wool and flax or wool and linen together. We Christians do this from time to time, finding bombs, helicopters and submarines in the Bible (particularly in Revelation). We use analogy to interpret the Word of God and it can completely distort the actual meaning as well as the spiritual truth behind it. This can be dangerous and has to be done very carefully. Analogy or Qiyas in Islam is a legitimate method of interpreting texts of the Qur'an or Hadiths. It allows for a more flexible way to adjust Islam to the changing circumstances of modern living.

CHAPTER 5
Islamic Equivalents

By using ideas already in Islam we can illustrate spiritual and biblical truths. We can also use Islamic ideas to teach our Muslim friends just how far short Islam falls with regard to reasonable human behaviour.

The Place of Jihad in Religion

All wars have used religion to justify themselves. War is bound up in the heart of man, no matter what culture, race, people or tongue you look at. The nature of man is to fight, kill and argue with his neighbour. Islam actually codifies war and gives it a raison d'être. The word 'Jihad' means exertion and by extension has come to mean holy war in the defence of Islam. There have been times when Muslims have felt threatened either by outside forces, such as the Crusaders or, more often than not, by Muslims who disagree with each other, such as the Jihads of West Africa, which were wars fought by Muslims against other Muslims with whom they disagreed.

Man is the most destructive force ever created and millions have died at his hands. Whole tribes have disappeared when man has invaded their territories. Look at Genghis Khan, whose army, when he died, killed every living thing that came across their path on their way back to bury him in Mongolia. This is not to mention the many who died when he was alive. His zeal was fuelled by a sense of call or mission. He felt God, his God, had called him to conquer the world. This sentiment is not exclusive to Genghis Khan; many world leaders have fought and killed in order to establish the law of their God on the earth. It is the most natural human thought justifying evil actions by doing them in the name of God. Look at the Crusades of the 12th century. In the name of Christ (and in disobedience to Christ) the European forces attacked Byzantium

and Islam in greed for land for their sons. Some no doubt felt that
the church should liberate Jerusalem and other holy cities from the
Turkish armies that had conquered them, but they did so in disobedience to Christ. They had to use Christ's name because the people
needed to know that what they were doing was permitted and so
leaders used His name wrongly. Christ Himself taught 'love your
enemy'. The resulting imposition of suffering and death only shows
the weakness of any religion. Even Christianity can become a vehicle of fear, a system imposed upon people through fear or superstition. We always have to remember that our present relationship
with Christ is more important than ecclesiastical structures or stric-
tures. This would be true of the Christianity of the Crusades or the
central teachings of Islam. In these various historical examples men
were afraid of being asked hard questions and thus exposing to all
the fact that they could not stand the test of close examination. Love
is actually a stronger force than fear and can cause people voluntarily to follow and do great deeds. If motivated by fear people
leave or turn against their leader once that fear is removed. A
religion or an empire held together by fear will die when that fear
is taken away.

The other issue is that fear will limit that society in its ability
to be creative. A child who is afraid to displease its parents and
seeks to fulfil every wish will never develop into a free, creative
individual. Fear crushes the human spirit. True Jihad is to struggle
against sin, Satan and self as we see in the example that Jesus
Christ gave us. Paul tells of his own struggle of fighting against his
own body in order to bring it under subjection to Christ.

The Jews looked for the judge Messiah (a human judge, that is)
and so they rejected the suffering servant manifestation. They wanted
freedom from the oppressive Romans and global domination for
themselves as followers of the Messiah. This desire is common to
any political or religious leader; all want to conquer the world by
force. Ever since nations have existed and to this very day the mark
of human desire is to conquer and rule others. When Jesus rejected
their image of what the Messiah should do at that time, the Jews
were deeply disappointed. On Good Friday they waved Him into
Jerusalem expecting conquest. By Saturday they were calling "crucify Him". When leaders do not conform to their followers' expec-

tations, they get removed; it is a clear example of man unable to live in freedom and his need to dominate and try to control others. It is the mark of a man-made religion.

Inspiration or Wahy

Ahmad Deedat says that the Bible is not inspired by God but that the Qur'an is. The problem lies not in the fact that he is right or wrong, although we will discuss this later, but that his idea of inspiration is different from what the Bible actually claims for itself. It is childish to establish a set of ideas outside the Bible and then claim they do not fit. We can illustrate this with the story of the man who beat his donkey because it never won a race amongst horses. It was never made to run fast but to carry burdens each day. The Bible never claims that it is a copy of a book on a table in heaven. That idea is totally foreign to its nature. Inspiration in Islam means that there exists in heaven a book, which was brought down, piece by piece over a period of time to a human being. The man then passes it on, without interference, to others who memorise it. Finally it is collected and collated into one book.

In fact many Muslim scholars are having difficulty even with this traditional view of the Ulema (see 'The 23 Years' by Ali Dashti, etc.). Muhammad told his followers that the words he spoke were revealed to him by God. Obviously all those original people who were given pieces of the Qur'an are now dead and we cannot check with them to see if what we have today is accurate. We therefore have to trust the original copies and documents that they wrote. However these were destroyed by Uthman when he collected all the pieces together to make one book. Destroying the pieces meant that no more arguments could arise. We therefore have to trust either the copies of early Qur'an's (not the originals) or sayings in the Hadith which vouch for its faithful collection, or the actual good character of the chain (Isnad) of people that passed it on to others.

There is a great cartoon of Charlie Brown playing baseball. On having been struck out he walks back to the dressing room complaining to himself: "I can't understand it, I was so sincere".

Sincerity and good character are no test of accuracy. Would you trust a navigator or a pilot in an aircraft to fly you simply on the basis of his good character? In fact, Aisha, Muhammad's wife, said that the rats had eaten some of the Qur'anic parchments she had stored in a box under her bed. Accuracy and completeness cannot be proved. Thus the Islamic view of transmission from heaven to earth via a human agent does not give us much hope of an accurate text.

The Jews also believed in inspiration. They believed God moved on the prophets' hearts and minds and they spoke truth and foretold events to come, for instruction and as a warning. They also wrote accurately of historical events, not for us to copy them but that we might learn from them. The record of David's adultery with Bathsheba (2 Samuel chapters 11 &12) is not recorded for us to copy, but to take warning that God sees all. The Old Testament truly knows the prophets as Mundhir (warner of wrath to come), Rasul (messenger of God to His people Israel) and Nabi (prophet of future events). Despite their not understanding them fully, but being faithful in their utterances, 39 books in the Old Testament were written by kings, shepherds and generals over 5,000 years, and across many countries, yet they all agree with one another. That is to say that they are telling the people what God's character is, what He wants His people to do and be and, at times, encouraging and comforting them during periods of oppression. In other words, God works in and through historical events, displaying His nature for all to see. In telling Israel to do something, He is not giving all people everywhere a model to follow but a revelation about His own Holy character. It would be true to say that the central purpose (or one of them) of the Bible is to reveal God's character to mankind so that they might know who He is, how He works and what He requires of man. His "laws", as it were, flow from His character. Thus the command not to kill, steal or lie stem from His character and not from His command not to do those things. Thus Christ fully reveals God in all His glory and characteristics.

There are occasions when prophets are allowed to hear God's voice audibly in order to receive specific instruction of great importance. Moses receiving the 10 Commandments is one such case, Exodus 20. All the New Testament writers, and there are 27 books in that collection, were aware that what they wrote and taught was an extension and an interpretation of what had already been received in the Old Testament under the supreme guidance of the Holy Spirit (called in Arabic 'Ruh Muqaddas'). Even here we must be careful in the use of semantics. By saying 'Holy Spirit' our Muslim friends would understand us to mean the angel Gabriel. Great and lofty as an angel is, he is still not God. Christians believe the Holy Spirit is in fact God. Being God, He is able to guide and oversee the writing down of words for the purpose of transmitting the ideas of God. He uses men's minds and personalities and events to communicate an accurate message. However, this is not the full understanding that we have of inspiration.

The Jewish view of inspiration was that God spoke through his prophets, He visited them in dreams and worked through historical events to reveal His true nature and His will. They also believed that God guided the writing down of events, ideas and thoughts so that they truly reflected the nature of God and His will. Neither did inspiration leave out the fact that other cultures had aspects of truth such as the Proverbs that were collected by David or Solomon. The act of collection was inspired and false proverbs were omitted.

John's gospel gives us a deeper understanding of inspiration. John 1[1] says that God created the world by speaking. He made man by his command (speech). His word then took human form in order that we might have a perfect and clear understanding of God's nature. A poor understanding of God's holiness hinders our ability to live in a changing world. We try to control events in life by making rules, hoping to control people and events. By seeking only to follow the written rules we yearn for a re-creation of past eras which can never be re-created. In Islam even rules can be avoided or made empty by the use of certain measures. There is a legal way of doing something that is illegal.

When Ahmad Deedat says the Bible is not the inspired word of God, what he is actually saying is that it does not conform to his view and understanding of what inspiration is. I agree it certainly does not conform to his view of what inspiration should be, but that does not make it a true representation of what true inspiration is. It only goes to show his own ignorance and inability to be objective and reasonable.

Seal of the Prophets, Khatam al Nabia

We would all want the latest model of TV, or edition of book, or car model. We like to think that ours is the genuine and final issue. So also in religion. We all like to think that our group has the final and most authoritative revelation from God. Let us consider the issues here.

First of all let us be honest and admit that having the final revelation can (though it does not always) make us proud and look down on others who have earlier models. This focus on a person is common in all religions. It can also detract from actually looking to God Himself. It is only to God that we are to look for inspiration and guidance. Thus we find that Jews look to Moses, Moslems to Muhammad, Mormons to Joseph Smith, Ahmadiyans to Gulam Ahmad, Christian Scientists to Mary Baker Eddy, Hindus to Sai Baba and so on and so forth. Christians, of course, look to Jesus and believe Him to be a visible revelation of the one and only God. This is where they would be accused of being exclusive and narrow minded, because their view excludes a revelation in these other men.

For the irreligious or earnest seeker it seems like a supermarket of choices and all claim to be the best and the latest, and so we see the tensions and conflicts that this variety can cause amongst communities.

In Deuteronomy 18 it says that if anyone comes claiming to be a prophet, test his claim. How are we to test the claims of each of these in order to arrive at a final choice? In Berea (Acts 17[11]) the people were commended for being ones who searched, tested and proved the scriptures to see if the things told to them were true. Indeed in Isaiah God even says "Come, let us reason together ..." (Isaiah 1[18]). Many of my Muslim friends complain that they accept Moses, Abraham, Noah, David and all the Old Testament prophets along with Jesus. Seemingly unfairly, Christians do not generally accept Muhammad as a prophet. They ask me why.

My reply is as follows. Firstly because so many people claim to be a prophet we must test and prove if anyone really is. In the Upper Nile areas of Sudan there have literally been hundreds of men and women claiming to be prophets. Even in Muhammad's time many claimed to be inspired. In our own time Jim Jones led hundreds to their death in Guyana as a false prophet. Jesus Himself warned us that after Him there would come many false prophets. Muhammad implied the same thing when he said he was the seal of the prophets, i.e. that none after him would be true. So what are the tests?

1) Prophecy means just that, telling the future.

2) Prophets are also messengers of God and God acts on their behalf. They do miracles, extraordinary feats that normal men cannot do. In both cases Muhammad states in the Qur'an that he himself had neither a prophecy nor did miracles, but prophets to be true prophets must speak and act in ways that confirm them as men of God. They must conform to what truth we have of God and His ways. They confirm previous scriptures.

Jesus said through His revelation to John in the book of Revelation that to add to or take away from the revelation would result in the following: "God shall add to him the plagues that are written in the book" Rev 22[18]. He was to be the final revelation to man. For any other man or woman to come and state that he is adding to the message was not acceptable. Thus Muhammed is excluded in the words of Jesus and the New Testament.

Thus we have a problem in that;

· Many, even to this day, claim to be prophets.

· Jesus claimed to be the final word of God.

· Muhammad, 600 years later, claimed he was a prophet and the last that God would send.

Let us test these claims;

Has Muhammad any extraordinary feats to his credit? He did create a new tribe 'Umma' from many tribes and made the Arabs united, but surely many men, including Alexander the Great and Genghis Khan, have done the same thing, only to have their new empire disintegrate soon after their death. After Muhammad's death there were the 'Ridda wars', a time of civil war when Arabs left Islam. Consequently, they had to be brought back into the faith.

He gave them a new law to live by, but then so did the
Pharaohs of Egypt, the Great Persians, Rome and, of course, Lek
of the Albanians. All great civilisations have been lawgivers. In
fact, Muhammad defined only six laws, all of which are common
to all mentioned. The Sharia developed later. In the Hadith it
claims that he did do miracles (Bukhari). However, many dispute
one Hadith against another. Some, like Joseph Schacht discount all
Hadith and, in fact, they were not recorded until 200 years after
Muhammad. In the Qur'an Muhammad speaks against the
Hadith that claims he did miracles " ... I do no miracles". Q6
(Cattle) and Q17[61.]

Of course, our Muslim friends cannot agree with what the Qur'an
stands on and have to introduce extra Qur'anic materials in order
to bring both the person of Muhammad and Islam up to at least the
same level as Judaism.

The Qur'an itself is said to be a sign. What kind of a sign?
Beautiful poetry we are told. Indeed many love to hear the recitation of the Qur'an when done so by skilled 'Hafez', those who have
memorised the Qur'an. This overlooks the grammatical mistakes in
the Arabic as well as the lost meaning of some of the words. In the
Jahiliyya (pre-Islamic Arabia) there were many poets and sages.
Indeed, Muhammad had some of them assassinated for writing poems
against himself.

As an Englishman I love to hear poetry in my own tongue.
Great poetry, if this test is allowed, would produce many more
'inspired' books if the only test were their beauty, rhyme and
rhythm.

The rapid conquest of the Byzantine and Persian world by the
Muslim armies has often been seen as a proof of God's blessing.
Are we to allow Hitler's conquest of Europe, Alexander's conquest
of Asia, Timurlane's conquest of Central Asia, to be a proof of God
with those people ? Obviously not. Is there a greater conqueror than
Genghis Khan? Surely with no army, no weapons, no command to
kill, Jesus Christ's conquest from Rome in the West all the way to
China in the East is an amazing feat - worthy of a wider reading of
his teachings, a closer examination of who He was and a willingness to join His crusade of love more readily.

Who was Jesus Christ?

Finally the word 'Christ' (Greek) or 'Messiah', 'Mesih' (Hebrew, Arabic) has a very well defined meaning in the Jewish books. It means the anointed one. In Isaiah 9[6-7] He is called Mighty God and Everlasting Father. This Messiah or Mesih has two definitions in the Old Testament. They indicated the two functions that the Messiah would fill: Ruler and Judge e.g. Isaiah 9[6:] "... and the government shall be upon his shoulders" and Suffering Servant, as in Psalm 27: "Do not hide your face from me, do not turn your servant away in anger" v 9 and Isaiah 53 "Surely he took up our infirmities and carried our sorrows, yet we considered him stricken by God, smitten by him and afflicted" (v 4).

In fact this line of thought introduces us to one of our tests for prophecy. There are over 300 prophecies in the Old Testament about who the Messiah is, His role in life, how He would live and die and what the purpose of His coming was. Jesus both fulfilled all these prophecies and gave prophecies Himself, some of which have now come to pass, such as the fall of Jerusalem, Matt 23. Some wait to be fulfilled, i.e. Matt 24[14].

His first coming to the earth was to suffer for our sins, setting us free by being 'Qurban', sacrifice, for us. On His return He comes as Ruler and Judge whom we should be ready to receive properly.

His signs also indicate who He was: He raised the dead, opened the eyes of the blind, stilled the storms at sea, healed the lepers and obeyed to the point of voluntarily allowing mortals to kill Him. There is overwhelming evidence of His miraculous powers which attest to His character. So we are faced with a decision. Do we accept Jesus or Muhammad? Who had the evidence that they truly were who they claimed to be? These are choices the sincere seeker must look at and come to a decision. His eternal future rests on this. For a further study of this the reader should refer to one or more of the many books written concerning the evidence, from a popular book like "Ben Hur", which was supposed to be a book written disproving the resurrection and through the weight of evidence came to be a statement of the resurrection, through to "The Robe" by Henryk Sienkiewicz, "Evidence that Demands a Verdict" by McDowell, and many others.

If I had buried a friend in the ground and three days later he walked into my house looking for me, I should be shocked. Then if he told me that I should change my house location because a storm was to come that would sweep my house away, I should listen and obey him very carefully. His return from the grave was important enough for him to come and warn me. So also we must listen to the voice of Jesus Messiah, since He also rose from the dead and warns us of coming judgement on sin and His offer of forgiveness. So seriously did the Roman authorities consider the story of the resurrection of Jesus that they passed a law that made grave robbery punishable by death. They thought his disciples had stolen Jesus' body in order to fulfil the claim that He would rise. Some still believe that interpretation, but it does not stand up to serious objective investigation.

But what was it that transformed these frightened, cowed disciples into bold preachers and why did they suffer persecution and death, even their families, if it was in fact they themselves who stole His body? They overturned the Roman empire without anger, without killing and without fighting through another power, the power of Jesus being inside them by His Spirit. It was only later that Christianity became a state religion and that process killed its spirit. The true 'Khatam al Nabia', seal of the Prophets, is found in Revelation 22[18] and refers to the Word of God Himself: "I warn everyone who hears the words of the prophecy of this book: If anyone adds anything to them, God will add to him the plagues described in this book. And if anyone takes words away from this book of prophecy, God will take away from him his share in the tree of life and in the holy city, which are described in this book."

The Ideal Man, Insan al Kamil or the illogicality of fundamentalism

Jesus was never a Prime Minister. He never rode a bike, cooked a hamburger or had an X-ray. Yet millions want to be like Him. So what does going back to the fundamentals mean? How can a man, woman or system be a model for the world of today? Obviously by wanting to be like Jesus we do not mean to copy Him exactly in all that He did. Yet in Islam this is the very doctrine of the Insan al

Kamil, the perfect man, the model of all and every society, Muhammad. He is the cornerstone of Islam. Islam stands or falls on the Qur'an and Muhammad. He is in fact the role model for all Muslims everywhere, they consciously or unconsciously emulate him. Thus we find similarities between his life and practice and the way Muslims react today. In fact this came about because Muslim soldiers and rulers took over the rule of government of conquered lands. Lacking in guidance, they did two related things. Firstly, they left in place those laws and customs they found in the territories they won, as long as they did not directly clash with what guidance they did have. Secondly, they islamicised those laws and actions via the Hadith. These stories purport that Muhammad had already said and done certain things that foreshadowed those laws anyway and so they were in fact Islamic laws. He therefore is elevated to the role of a living revelation and a model for all Muslims to follow - Insan al Kamil, the perfect man. Thus in marrying Aisha at 6 years of age he legalises child marriage. He also had a red beard and many today dye their beards red to be like him.

This process of elevating Muhammad to the point of being inspired in his actions as well as his words makes him an equal with scripture and was legitimised by injunctions in the Qur'an to obey God and his prophet (Q57[7] Hadid). Not only in what he is telling the community, but also each and every action now becomes of value for guidance. In Mecca he was mocked and scorned. Merchants paid poets to write satirical poems mocking his claim to prophethood and inspiration. On gaining power in Medina he sent assassins to kill these poets. Thus, when Ghadaffi or Khomeini sends assassins to kill his enemies or even writers like Rushdie, they are in fact following a model set before them. They are being totally consistent with their faith. How different is our Lord, who from the cross cried "Father, forgive them, they know not what they do" Luke 23 v 34.

In the year 624 AD Muhammad broke the Arab custom of a truce during the month of Ramadan and took hostages. The violation of an international commitment to honour Embassy territory is justified by Muhammad's example in his actions. Thus the storming of the American Embassy in Tehran can be viewed as following the example set by Muhammad.

Salvation history is the story of the founder and his immediate associates and gives a living example of how the religion is to be interpreted and understood. Salvation history is extremely important for all religions. It is the breeding ground of the faith and purest interpretation of the faith in that it is the first case of the faith being acted out and becomes a scenario for understanding what the original mouthpiece understood, and thus what God intended.

In Muhammad's case there are two different locations to relate to, Mecca and Medina. In Mecca he was a voice crying in the wilderness, calling for reform, worship of one God, with social concern for widows and orphans. A man of peace and persuasion. In Medina his changed circumstances are preceded by several major events in his life.

i)   The death of his first wife, Khadija

ii)   The death of his uncle, who had protected him from the Meccans.

iii) His failure after 13 years of ministry to win over the majority of the townspeople.

iv)   The resulting rejection causes him to flee for his life in 622 AD-now called the "Hijrah".

This 'Hijrah' or flight has become a symbol of hope for many Muslim revolutionaries like Khomeini, Al Afghani, and even Idi Amin. Following their banishment they could look back to 622 AD and take hope that they would also return in the same way, to power, as Muhammad does after that time.

The psychological impact of these two events on Muslims today must not be underestimated. When Muslims make up a minority in a society they tend to be peaceful and appeal to logical debate and reason to promote their faith à la Meccan period. On becoming a significant percentage of a community they move over to Medinan mentality in taking up the sword and seeking to overthrow the host community and impose Sharia law. This can be seen in Lebanon and Sudan and could well be seen in Europe in days to come.

Thus a seemingly peaceful community is transformed at a certain stage of its evolution into a warlike state set against all perceived non-Islamic forms of government and laws, not because those laws are unjust or irrelevant but simply because they do not conform to the model presented to the Islamic community in their salvation history. They would claim denial of their rights if they couldn't practise their laws in a foreign land.

The role of Muhammad is limited even in the Qur'an and Hadith, so a third doctrine is brought into play: Ijma (consensus of opinion by the leading clergy). Muslim desire for martyrdom is a result of salvation history, the account of how they came into being (perceived or otherwise). This is not to say that they should be true or historically correct. The important thing is that the adherents believe they are true. The early Muslim battles meant that believers were lost and they have been immortalised as examples of men of faith. This gives rise in the 20th Century to men and women wishing to emulate these 'martyrs', hence the human bombs in Lebanon and Palestine, and suicide squads.

These are not the result of some fanatical group but the example they have within their own history. We must not look at the members of a religion, for all have their 'bad eggs', but at its founders. Just as Christians would look to Christ, the apostles and the early church fathers for an interpretation of what the faith meant and how it should be practised, not to subsequent evil men who used Christ for their own ends.

But does not all religious belief rely upon salvation history? Of course it does and we must recognise that modelling is a most powerful stimulant to behaviour. Are not Christianity, Hinduism, Mormonism and the rest all guilty of this approach to revelation? Yes, but because of the peaceful non-violent model of Jesus this does not produce a violently reactionary movement. There have been Christian fanatics and the Crusades are a good example of that. However, this was in direct disobedience both to the example and the teachings of Jesus. Although led by sincere Christians, the Crusades were the antithesis of all that Jesus taught and suffered for.

Surely it would be unreasonable that our society should run on these lines. If we were to give in to every enemy when invaded, there could never be a safe, secure, stable populace. Any tribe or sect could overthrow ordered society. True, so here we must make some clear distinctions.

Firstly, the Crusaders could have reacted against the Arab/Turk/ Kurdish invasion of Byzantium through political alliances without resorting to calling it the will of God. The problem was that mediaeval men saw no distinction between church and state. Jesus separated the two, since He sought to build His kingdom in the hearts of man, but is that not rather idealistic and impractical? Does not man need a model for government? Yes and no. He needs to know how to act mercifully, but God gave man the freedom to build his own society and to defend that society against destruction. He gave rules to punish evil doers and murderers and the right to raise taxes to pay for the defence of the realm.

Such is the horror of war and killing to the followers of Christ that it has produced strong pacifist movements within civilisation. On the other hand, others can see the need to defend themselves and they consider the use of war as a last resort. The line separating self-defence from hatred is so thin that Christians have debated for centuries the idea as to whether there can be such a thing as a just war. All men are of one origin (Acts 17) and so they tend to act in a similar way. It is possible to see a commonality in all religions and religious experience. In one aspect there is very little difference between the actions of men under Islam, Christianity or Hinduism. Christianity as a religion is man-made just as all other religions are man-made and so also incorporate man's aspirations, fears, world view, culture and political needs. The fact is that Jesus never brought, created or intended to form a new religion. His central message was forgiveness, as seen in "the woman at the well", "the prodigal son" and ultimately the cross. Islam regulates and legitimises conflict, but Jesus' word brings all forms of offence to a stop by His teaching on forgiveness. Wars have been fought for territory and resources, over insults received and injustices real or perceived and there is enough evidence to show that neighbour cannot get along with neighbour. By first trying war, even regulating it, war is perpetuated. Blood revenge amongst Albanians and Pathans is legendary. Often killing takes place long after the original insult or offence has been forgotten and it has become a thing of family honour to perpetuate the clash. The salvation history of the founders of Islam is one of murder, war and assassination. Umar and Uthman both died at the hands of an assassin; Ali's sons were killed fighting the then rulers of the community after their father was killed trying to put down a revolt. All the Shia Imams were either killed with the sword or poisoned. Without resorting to the sword Islam could never have become established as a religious community outside of Medina. In the Christian faith it is very different. Christ allowed Himself to be taken to the cross and willingly gave His life for us. He did not fight to protect himself from his enemies.

When Muhammad moved to Medina (Yathrib) he found a number of Jewish tribes. Some he had to overcome but one tribe remained neutral, the Jews at Khaybar. He killed and enslaved them and imposed upon them the status of 'Dhimmi' or subjected peoples. He allowed them to carry on cultivating the oasis, provided they gave him half of their produce; he could break his contract with them at any time and expel them as he wished. They were to provide assistance to the Muslim forces, but were not allowed to bear arms. In addition they were to make space in their synagogues for the Muslims. This agreement was to become the model granted by all Arab conquerors upon their subjected peoples. It was an agreement by a strong party imposed upon another party without their approval. This Dhimmi status has been imposed wherever Muslim armies have overrun another people. It must be stated, however, that it was not the Muslims who invented the Dhimmi laws which governed the example that Muhammad had set. It was in fact Byzantine law and custom that the Arabs took over. The Greek church in Muslims lands died under the very laws that they had invented to persecute others.

Given that the world is divided into Dar al Harb, or the house of war, and Dar al Islam, the house of Islam, there is a permanent state of war between Muslims and all who have not come under their rule. This includes Europe and all other non-Islamic nations. There will be a constant agitation by immigrant peoples to overturn the existing structures, establish Islam and subject the host peoples to Dhimmi status. The sad thing is that many of these people flee from Muslim states because they cannot stand the oppression they themselves live under, only to be brought back under Islam by their leaders. Even just recently the late Prof. Siddiqi restated that the Fatwa or ruling on the writer Salman Rushdie stands. Siddiqi was the head of a so-called Islamic Parliament, which seeks to be an alternative government in the UK to the legally constituted one established by the majority. For them the status of non-Muslims is either death or Dhimmi status, which is still in existence in places like Iran, Sudan, Egypt and Algeria today.

CHAPTER 6

The Need for Cultural Awareness

One Sunday morning my sons went to a local Bible class. There were some 200 in the class and most went to the local Grammar schools. There in the classroom was a lad with a black leather jacket, 'bovver' boots, tight blue jeans and coloured hair. Embarrassment gripped the room. Who would be bold enough to witness to this boy? On turning round they were surprised to find the word "Jesus" written in silver studs right across his shoulders. He loved the Lord Jesus but dressed like the rest of his friends in the neighbourhood that he came from. Jesus himself told us not to judge on outward appearances but to judge righteous judgement. Sometimes our values get all rolled up into our culture.

Of all the passages in the Bible that speak the most clearly about the importance of the cultural context regarding communication, Paul's letters to Corinth and Philippi are the strongest. In 1 Corinthians 9[19-23] we read of his desire to get alongside and to empathise with those he is seeking to communicate to. Occasionally in missionary stories we come across men and women who also have acted in this way and drawn "fire" from other believers. Other workers find it a threat, since it exposes their lack of security in leaving their own culture and being free enough to identify with an alien one. Hudson Taylor took on the dress of a Chinese Mandarin and David Brainard lived with the Indians and came in for much misunderstanding and criticism from fellow workers.

I well remember travelling in the early days with an OM team in India. George Verwer led us on an outreach from Bombay northwards to Calcutta. En route we passed through Varanasi, the holy city of the Hindus. During that time it was the holy festival of Holi. It was enormous fun to see the packets of paint being flung left and right, all of us becoming multi-coloured in the process. Identification, acceptance and a willingness to mix meant that the local people,

Hindus and Muslims alike, were ready to listen to what we had to say. Another example was that of Sam Yeghnazar, who moved into work with the Bible Society in Beirut and immediately began to produce materials that related to the people of Lebanon. He was always saying "... the message we want to give in the packaging they want to receive it in ...". Paul's concern was that the messenger did not put people off considering the message. To many non-Christians, the way we have formerly 'done' evangelism has been offensive. Of course, the danger in anything is that you go too far and compromise. That's what I find so exciting about new approaches in presenting the gospel. We have to be thoroughly biblical and yet creative in the way we do things. I have come into great areas of freedom by being exposed to other cultures, although there is still much to learn. I realise just what a jewel we have in the gospel and that there is much left to man to explore and create; this freedom has been given by God Himself and I believe He delights in seeing His children be creative. Issues like dress, manners, customs and food are all important to a people. It is what makes them what they are, but they are open to change and acceptance or rejection as cultures change. Should the missionary take on these aspects of other cultures? There will be disagreement, but on the whole each person must be persuaded in his own mind and spirit. To some taking your shoes off in a mosque is seen to be a compromising act. To others it is irrelevant and can be done to accomplish a greater good.

Just how many missionary women have worn the Islamic veil in order to minister to Muslim women? Maybe we should even ask the question "should they?"

Another passage of Paul's is a commentary on the life of the Lord Jesus. In Philippians 2[5-8] he gives us the ideal model for the way we ought to do our work. Christ became a man and humbled himself, thus identifying with His creation even to the extent of dying on a cross as a criminal. This was in order to bring us up into the presence of the Father, an incredible act of love. How many people ministering to Punks and Skinheads dress like them? Are we capable of getting down to where people are, putting them at ease and saying: "I love you just the way you are"?. This does not mean that we also identify with their sin. One man I know drank heavily in order to reach some Mongols that he was nurturing. This was going too far, crossing the "line". He felt that if he drank as they did they would accept him and therefore the message he brought, but, of course, the message he was giving was distorting the very message he wanted to give - a real problem - and he has gone on to be out of step with the church and with many other believers in his ministry. Technically he is brilliant in what he does, but his life is a mess. There must be maturity, wisdom and balance. Balance is seemingly always a difficult thing to achieve. This concept of iden- tification is perfectly shown in Paul's attitude to winning the Jews. In Acts 15 the church leaders came together in order to settle an open debate. The question was: how do Gentiles become Chris- tians? As always, they looked to themselves in order to find a model and tried to develop a theology from their own experience, always a dangerous thing to do. They had become Christians by going through the rituals of being Jews first. To them it also fol- lowed that the Gentiles should go via the same route: that the Gentiles ought to be circumcised as they had been and thus keep the Jewish law before they could be accepted as Christians. This desire to replicate our own experience in others or judge others' experience in the light of our own is a great mistake. God deals with and meets all of us where we are as we are. He loves us without change and is only anxious to bring us fully into his family. Thus the seed sown and germinated brings its own fruit. Paul stood against this and the Council settled the matter in chapter Acts 15[19]. However, in Acts 16[1-3], Paul seems to go against all that he has been fighting for by taking Timothy and circumcising him. Now look at the text more closely. In verse 3 it says "for the sake of the Jews in that place". A perfect example of his not wanting the messenger to become a stumbling block to the hearers of the message. Paul practises all things to all men in order to win some.

Many of our church people fail to relate to the people that live all around them. After about three years we all lose our unsaved friends and live in a world that has only Christian contacts. How many of us are at home with unbelievers and comfortable in their presence? Do we enjoy them and have the maturity and security to be able to separate them from their sinful habits? Here again some of those habits are sinful simply because they do not fit our scheme of things. They are often cultural sins, class sins, but not moral sins.

It is much the same in Muslim work. We must discern what is acceptable, what is unacceptable and also what is perfectly natural. This may differ from person to person and we must be ready for others to disagree with us. I know some Dutch Christians who would say that if you take your shoes off before going into a mosque you are showing respect to the spirits in that mosque. Thus they would never do it.

I personally find this not a problem and the best conversations and times of witnessing have been when I have been in a mosque, shoes off, with my Bible. The Muslims feel at home and not threatened. I feel comfortable because "greater is He that is in you than he that is in the world" and so we can gently and wisely talk about biblical issues even inside a Mosque.

The use of Form and Structure

Christian workers have discovered that many Muslims are not as resistant to the gospel as they are to the western communicator or western forms of worship. When they are given opportunities to worship in their mother tongue and culturally congenial forms, they do so. Since some of you will want to experiment in this area; a great deal of care should be taken as to what forms are used;

There are Islamic forms of practices that are totally unacceptable and unredeemable in Christian worship. Examples are listed in the table following.

There are Islamic forms and practices that lend themselves to Christian worship. One should take great care, if they are used, to make sure they are fully and faithfully filled with Christian content.

Finally, there are those multitudes of cultural forms that are relatively neutral. They have to do with lifestyle and could be retained. (Some would maintain nothing is 'neutral'. This may be true, but no culture will be totally redeemed this side of the return of Christ). Don McCurry developed this chart of values for the seminars he used to give.

Unacceptable Forms	Facilitating Forms	Neutral Forms
· Kissing the Black Stone of the Kaaba	· Prayer postures	· Dress styles
· Reciting that part of the Credo which confesses Muhammad as the prophet of God	· Mosques as places of prayer	· Shaving habits; beards
	· Taking off shoes in the place of worship	· Eating habits
· Pilgrimage to Mecca	· Muslim hymns adapted in praise of Christ	· Exercise (walking habits)
· Unqualified endorsement of the Qur'an	· Reverence for the Word of God	· Visiting of friends in the evenings
· Use of Qur'anic verses as magic to ward off evil	· Memorisation of Scripture	· Design of houses
· Consulting Muslim holy men for magic potions for problems	· Early morning, noon and evening prayers	· Toilet habits
· Polygamy	· Caring for the poor	· Educational systems
· Jihad or Holy War in the cause of Islam	· Practice of fasting	· Washing before prayers
· Sensuous concept of Paradise	· Certain Muslim festivals if properly adapted	· Style of gardens
		· Art forms - rugs, mosaics, pottery, music, and so forth
		· Art forms - rugs, calligraphy, architecture, mosaics, pottery, music, and so forth

Examples of Behaviour & Status: Don McCurry

The above listings are only some of the Islamic material that could be so handled. You may want to add to these columns as your knowledge of Islamic culture grows.

One of the purposes of this section is to show you that we do not have to reject everything Islamic or Muslim. There is much that can serve as a bridge to introducing biblical material. There is much that is praiseworthy and equally there is much that can be left alone. Understanding the principles involved can help you develop more effective approaches to your Muslim friends. Note carefully how valuable this becomes in the following case studies.

Finding new images to communicate old truths

The missionary was arguing with the Muslim layperson. "Unless you accept Jesus as the son of God you will go to hell" he cried. Yes, that actually was said. The Muslim just stuck his fingers in his ears, cried out "Allah Akbar" and walked away. End of conversation, end of communication and end of contact. What the Muslim heard the missionary saying was completely different from what the missionary was wanting to communicate. He wanted to get across the point that Jesus was Jehovah God, The Self-Existing One, the Creator of the universe. What the Muslim 'heard' him saying was that God has a wife called Mary, with whom he'd had intercourse resulting in Jesus. Blasphemous to both!

During a Christian Union (CU) Christmas party I sat next to an Iraqi student who had been attending the CU meetings all that year. He loved the singing, the fellowship and spiritual and moral atmospheres. The CU were perplexed because they could not get him to "make a decision" for Christ. They had asked me to look out for him. On sitting next to him I started bluntly by saying that I believed only in one God. He grabbed my hand and shook it vigorously. "You are the first Christian I have met that believes in one God" he said with relief. The CU had not understood his dilemma, or his cultural "screen" that all they did and said had to pass through. Being a Muslim and believing the Qur'an to be true, he thought he understood what Christians believed, because the Qur'an told him that they believed in three gods (Q. 5[76]). Another problem for him was that to accept that Christians believe in only one God was to say that Muhammad had made a mistake, thus threatening the whole basis of his faith. How much time and trouble has been caused by the communicator's not understanding what the listener was receiving. Words like *sin, grace* and *forgiveness* all have different meanings within an Islamic context. No wonder Jesus taught in parables and stories. No wonder He came down and showed us God (and the Word became flesh) and did not rely just upon human words to communicate eternal matters.

So how do you get the message across? Basically by trust, by taking and investing time to build a relationship, earning the right to speak before jumping in at the deep end and making all sorts of wrong and misleading errors. Once trust has been established, then meaningful and valuable communication can begin. This takes time and is against the normal way that we westerners do things. Better to be a friend over a period of time than to 'witness' once and end the contact. Help friends with their English, take them to a zoo or a picnic, offer to help with Government red tape that may be confusing to them. Visit them not only at special times like a birthday or funeral but also just as a friend.

There will be difficult and perplexing questions that they will ask. They are genuinely confused about the deity of Christ, the Trinity, the atonement for sin and the lack of law within Christianity. However, sometimes these questions are put to you as a smoke screen, an attempt to try to get you away from looking too closely at Muhammad's life and teachings. I believe many Muslims are really embarrassed about their leader's life and morals but to admit to a westerner that their Arab leader was wrong is almost unthinkable.

There is a growing number of books and pamphlets that give answers, both from the Bible and the Qur'an, about the questions Muslims raise. A list is given at the back of this book. Here are a few that I have found useful;

- The Qur'an: An Introductory Essay, by Theodore Noldeke.
- Christians Answer Muslims, by Gerhard Nehls
- Christians Ask Muslims, by Gerhard Nehls.
- Christian Reply to Muslim Objections, by Tisdall
- The Infallibility of the Torah and the Gospel, by Iskander Jadeed.

- The Cross and the Crescent, by Phil Parshall.
- Ishmael My Brother, by Anne Cooper.
- Sharing your Faith with a Muslim, by Abdul Haqq.

Here are a few thoughts along these lines:

The Trinity: All illustrations break down at some point. However, time is made up of three complete yet indivisible elements; past, present and future. If there is no past, then there can be no future. So God is three yet exists in a unity. This is in contradistinction to the God of Islam, who is a unit.

The Deity of Christ: Ask them if the Qur'an is eternal, has always existed or is created at some point in time. Most will reply that the Qur'an exists in heaven and is eternal. The greatest sin in Islam is to commit *shirk*, which is associating something with God. This teaching grew out of the opposition to the title 'Son of God'; God has no partners, no equals. So if He has no partners, how can God and the Qur'an co-exist? This is *shirk*. Now tell your friend when he answers that mystery; then you will help explain how God became a man. Remember Muslims believe Christians are making a man into a god. We believe that God (who in Islam is supposed to be able to do anything) became a man in order to communicate and take our place as the sin offering. The Qur'an states He became a flame in the bush before Moses, Q 27$^{7-9}$ (Ant). If He can appear as a flame why not as a man?

The Cross: Probably the greatest offence in Islam is the cross. How, they ask, can anyone bear the punishment for another's sins? The Muslim cannot accept that somebody actually died for another's sins. Muslims think this is illogical and unfair; man must bear his own punishment. I was preaching outside a mosque in Ahmedabad in Gujarat State, India, with an audience of 200. I recounted one of the stories about the end of the world told in the traditions (Hadith). It says that on the day of judgement God will call all men to cross the bridge Sirat, from earth to heaven. It is narrow as a hair and as sharp as a razor. Any with sin will fall off the bridge and the angels will pour molten lead into their ears, nose and mouth. I recounted the story with appropriate feeling and drama. Then I asked who amongst them will be able to cross the bridge? None moved. None put up their hand. By their own witness they were lost. It was at that point I pointed out the provision in the lamb of God who took our punishment and set us free.[1] This "lamb of God" took our place to satisfy an eternal law against sin. This often leads to accepting gospels and a search begins.

Muslims say that **the Bible has been changed**: This has to be taught, because, if they were to accept the Bible, then they would have to obey it and not the Qur'an. They read that Jesus said that after Him another comforter would come (John 14[16]). Who is the comforter? Most Christians will say this is the Holy Spirit but they say it was Muhammad. The fact that Muhammad's name is not in the New Testament proves that Christians have changed their book. If it has been changed, when was it changed, before Muhammad or after him? If before, then why does Muhammad exhort his followers to read the Bible? If after, then we have copies of the New Testament long before Muhammad's death that can be examined and shown to have never been changed. From the fact that we have so many versions it can easily be shown that the Greek and Hebrew have not changed. Rather, it is the meaning of the English language that changes according to the era. For example, years ago the word *gay* meant *happy*, now, of course, it often refers to one who is homosexual. In order that we may understand God's message for man, we must translate the meaning and not just the words into modern parlance.

Ahmad Deedat: This man is becoming a very popular figure in certain circles of Muslims. His ignorance and misrepresentation of Christianity are outstripped only by most Christians' ignorance of Islam. One of his favourite statements is that nowhere in the Bible does Jesus ever say He is God. Of course, this is not true, but most believers are shaken when they first hear this statement. Why is it in John 10[31] that the Jews pick up stones to kill him when he says "I and the Father are one"? It was because they knew He was presenting himself as God. Also at his baptism God the Father spoke from heaven, saying 'This is my beloved Son, with whom I am well pleased' Matt.3 v 17.

---

[1]The Dickens story of the 'Tale of Two Cities' is also a useful parable of how God saves man.

To the woman at the well in John 4 Jesus says He is the Messiah. The key, of course, is in what the Jews of his day understood the term 'Messiah' to mean. After the destruction of Jerusalem in 70 AD they gave the term a new meaning. Isaiah tells us He is called Everlasting Father, Prince of Peace. The Old Testament clearly portrays the Messiah as God come in the flesh to save His people. Edersheim's book 'The life and times of Jesus the Messiah' has a large section just on the verses in the Old Testament that refer to the Messiah and who He was.

Divisions in Christianity: Here many Christians hang their heads in shame. How can we have the truth when there are so many denominations in the church? Islam believes in oneness. Islam sees its system as being One God, one community, one faith. This is not a problem for me. I see the multiplicity of churches as reflecting God's creative nature. Nobody has all the truth and ever changing circumstances mean that the churches can change to reflect those changes. Life is vibrant and free. He gives us the freedom to create our own societies within certain bounds. No first century model is fossilised for us to copy. Islam has a tradition where Muhammad says that there will be 73 sects of Islam but only one will be the truth. The trouble is no one knows which one is the true one. There are more sects and groups than in Christianity, once you get to know of them.

To those who can learn to adapt and adjust to the changing cultures they have to minister in and to will come many thrilling experiences. They will gain many rich insights into biblical truth and be able to understand the mind of God and His word. Our God is the God of culture and His plan is for us to respect and enjoy them. Culture makes a multicoloured life for us and enables us to express ourselves and know who we are. Building a church that is relevant and has its own culture will produce a stable and powerful community.

CHAPTER 7
Modern Issues

Much of what we have been looking at deals with classical Islam, the Islam of ancient history and of the text books. There is, of course, the Islam that is adapting to today's world. This adaptation fundamentally started when the French, under Napoleon, invaded Egypt in 1798. Napoleon brought with him many scholars, engineers and teachers to try to discover and record what they were to find in that great and ancient land. In the process he introduced many of the new scientific developments of France and the West. Schools, factories, methods and approaches helped to make Egyptians aware of what was lacking in their own land. This began a process of assimilation and adaptation, as they sought to take advantage of the benefits of the West, yet keep an Islamic basis. By learning European languages and studying western writers and philosophers they began to respond and develop their own applications of the new ideas they were being exposed to. You will find Muslims who have been profoundly influenced by the following writers and you should be aware of both the issues and the background to these streams of thought.

One recurring problem that Muslims have faced is that of producing a definitive description of what Islam is. The same quandary exists in producing a definition of sin. Surah 5^{44-50} urges all Muslims to resist corrupt rulers, who do not judge according to what God sent down. There is great freedom for each to interpret what this means. The following are some of those thinkers who are important today and who influence Islamic development.

Sayyid Qutb of the Egyptian Brotherhood

For Qutb in Egypt it was a strict application of the Islamic form of family rather than the United Nations concept of nationhood. He rejected the nation of Egypt and stood for a greater vision of a united Islamic brotherhood. How he could ever suggest the governance of all Muslims globally without problem is difficult to see. This romantic idealism has rent Muslim communities ever since it began.

Qutb's vision of an Islamic interpretation of nationhood rather than the modern view of the nation state led to his execution by the Egyptian government in 1966. Rather than accepting the development of nationalism he returned to a 7th century view that he saw as the ideal model for all time. Obviously his view differs from that of other modern Islamic thinkers. He was a member of Ikhwan al Muslimun, currently waging war against the Egyptian government and responsible for the assassination of Sadat.

Unusually, he maintained that there was a literary artistry in the writing of the Qur'an, which suggests the role of the man Muhammad in the transmission of the Qur'an. This view collides with the view of a totally illiterate prophet and a celestial Qur'an untouched in its transmission to man. Of course, some welcomed this new development in Islamic thinking and saw the hope for a new wind of change in Islamic philosophy, but others saw it as a threat to the stability and inspiration once and for ever given to the world through the prophet.

Since Islam is seen to be a total system incorporating social, political and religious values, Qutb was inevitably drawn into conflict with the Egyptian government. To recover the original Islamic pattern as given by Muhammad to them in the 7th century (as understood by them) is the goal of all Islamic purists. They see that the purity of Islam has been lost by both unfaithful Muslims and the corrupting influence of the West and other philosophies. Governments stand or fall in their estimation according as to whether they express judgement as given in Allah's revelation in Surah 5[44]. There exists a spectrum of responses to secular authority by various Muslim movements, balancing a desire to impose their view of what the revelation requires with a need to avoid chaos and confusion in society.

Qur'anic injunctions which refer to specific circumstances in Muhammad's life are extrapolated to apply to all Muslim communities. This is because of the doctrine of obedience to God and His prophet. Qutb and others with the Umma can always claim a monopoly of decision on the Islamic community, because they purport to speak for pure Islam. Thus one group falls out with another - a recipe for internecine war.

It would not be right to go on without pointing out that salvation history propels Islam. Each Muslim school of thought is conscious of the Jahiliyya (times of ignorance, pre-Islamic Arabia) and the possibility of its sweeping return via corrupt governments. Thus they see themselves as (the only) guardians of Islam. They are consciously or unconsciously responding to the example of Muhammad in fighting all or any unbelief as they view it. Thus Muhammad, having set the example and put himself forward as a model for the Muslim, has unwittingly perpetuated conflict in the community. It is always easier to criticise those in government, since life never works out in the ideal way we all wish. Thus revolution and counter-revolution gyrate around Muslim lands. The Fatimids of North Africa in the 9th century ably criticised the Egyptian government whilst in opposition, but quickly crumbled once in power, taking on many of the sins of those they criticised.

This romanticism comes about partly because of an inadequate understanding of evil, and especially of evil in men. No amount of right belief or interpretation will allow for right action because of the weakness of will and perversity of heart in men. Their argument is to impose, as in Saudi Arabia, by use of religious policemen, strict adherence to Islamic law. Ways are always found around these restrictions. This naturally leads to pride and violence, they are the only ones who know the will of God and all others are 'Kafir' unbelievers. By setting out to impose this will on all others irrespective of convictions, a manifestation of the very spirit they set out to denounce occurs.

Muhammad's early works elevated 'Fitna' (dissension) in the community as an evil over individual crimes that people commit. Again Qutb falls into this sin, as he rebelled against the existing if not legitimate government of Egypt, thus bearing out Paul's words in Romans that "man is inexcusable in that he does what he judges in others". Christ's words about the man concerned about another with a mote in his eye, while being blind to the plank in his own eye, is an apt commentary on this situation.

We therefore need to identify several forces that play upon the Muslim community and to which they are forced to respond;

- That of being a minority in another country, e.g. India or UK.

- Secular pressure from the International community; e.g. being members of the UN.

- Interrelation with other Muslims who have often interpreted Islam in the light of their own cultural world view.

- Interrelation with other religions where other moral and ethical standards are seen to be superior to those that Islam espouses, for example in the areas of child marriages and monogamy.

It is interesting that the central theme of Christianity is to deal with the very issue that unravels Islam and any other religious idealism, namely the sinfulness of man and how he can be reconciled to God only through Jesus. Christianity is NOT about working out which rules apply to man and life but is a revelation of God to man about Himself and how man can have a warm and loving relationship with his maker. Religion tries to work out details such as dates, times, seasons and customs and makes them as if they are God given and for ever. Christ actually cuts the ropes of this limiting view of life and offers a new way forward based upon forgiveness.

Qutb's other failure is his inability (deliberate or otherwise) to take into account the non-Arab Muslim world, especially countries where Islam is a minority, such as is found in Malaysia, Thailand, India and many parts of Africa. His call for revolt against 'corrupt' non-Sharia government could only lead to frustration at least and elimination at worst, thus leading peaceful communities into suffering, war and conflict with their own governments. This did take place in West Africa during the 19th and 20th century Jihads. Muslim fought Muslim as one denounced the other as not being fully Muslim.

To understand why Muslims can be antagonistic towards Christians we need to understand the Muslim world view. In Islam there is no (or should not be any) separation of 'church' and state or, should we say, Mosque and state. Such separation is anathema to a Muslim, as he believes that Islamic law is from God and must therefore be obeyed. Religious freedom means freedom to be a

Muslim or suffer the consequences of being Dhimmi or second class people in a Muslim state.

Islam views western nations as Christian and what their governments do as the result of Christian actions. One of the pre-evangelism steps we have to assert is the true nature of Christ's mission - that He came to set individuals free and not to establish a theocratic state. We therefore must try to explain the concept of personal faith, which has as its root a moral and ethical code powered by spiritual realities. These, like dew drops, combine gently to form a larger society quietly to transform nations. If personal piety wanes and family quality declines, the nation is corrupted, no matter what laws or governments try to do.

Ali Shariati of Iran

Ali Shariati was born in 1933. He was a clear thinker and a political activist in Iran. To him God rules and man submits. There was no other option. He decried those who mimicked the West like the Qajar Shahs who were the Persian rulers prior to the Shah of Iran's family, the Pahlavis. To him the dynasty of the Shah of Iran was hopelessly lost in rootlessness and irreligion. To him the Sufi mystics of Persia were equally irrelevant, since they avoided vigorous action to change by retreating into pietism.

Whilst many Muslim scholars abhorred western ideologies, he saw no problem in studying in Paris (1959-64). He drew much from the thinking of Franz Fanon, who inspired the Algerian revolution. Thus sociological ideas fuelled his desire to liberate his view of true Islam and recast it to meet the needs of his Persia. Fanon's philosophy of violence found overtones in Muhammad's struggle against injustice, rejection and conquest over Arabian city states. Fanon saw the needs of society overriding individual freedoms, so that there could be corporate liberation, not unlike another German, Nietzsche. Thus *jihad* (Holy war) and a hatred of *fitnah* (dissimulation), two Islamic pillars, coincide with Fanon's world view. These Islamic 'tools' can legitimately be brought into the Islamic arena, being triggered by this interaction of western ideology.

Thus we see Islam constantly acting in reaction to its environment - in one sense a 'living faith', in that it is constantly being reinterpreted to respond to cultural, political and sociological trends, but can we not say this is also true of Christians? Yes, of course we can, but Christ did not give us a pattern and law to be followed for all time without changes. He gave us an eternal moral code and freedom to choose the type of government and law that is relevant and responsive to the needs of life, as long as it conforms to the law of love. Not only that, through the cross we have forgiveness which sets us free to be the people we are created to be. This freedom is best experienced in the personal development of the gifts and talents we have. Any oppression or crushing of the human spirit limits the discovery and use of talent which can be used to serve society. Psychosis and breakdown come from the oppression of the human spirit. Instead of playing an equal part in the workplace in medicine, art, law and other disciplines women are consigned to activities that men assume for them. There is a growing number of feminist writers like Sadawi and Mernissi who are both speaking out against this oppression by men and even going back to the Quranic sources for a reinterpretation of Islam.

Again, the Salvation History of Islam is appealed to in order to substantiate the use of power. The political nature of Islam, whether in the hands of Shariati, Afghani or Qutb, is doomed to promote conflict with both Muslim and non-Muslim institutions. It matters little whether he draws his inspiration from Muhammad or uses Muhammad to promote his own ideas. The nature and examples of Islam are interwoven. Contrast this with the Christ of the Cross, who, as a model, brings a stop to blood revenge by both teaching and example. Shariati died in 1977 in London in mysterious circumstances and is buried in Damascus.

There is a process of Christianisation of Islam taking place, out of all similitude of what was originally intended, by God or Muhammad. This has come about through the interaction of Islamic leaders with others outside the Islamic world. The elevation of Muhammad as the divine (in Shia terms) light of God, a process of deification, which many Sunnis have abhorred, is a direct Muslim response to the proclamation of Christ as God. Other institutions could be named, such as the Red Cross and the Red Crescent, democratic developments in these nations and many others.

Lacking a revelation from God and the power of the Word of God, they are drawn into a blasphemy they accuse others of and the creation of extracanonical literature that introduces man's thinking into Islam and overwhelms the simple vision of Muhammad completely, that there is only one God.

Muslims believe that Muhammad, being only the medium through which the message is delivered, has no responsibility for either its content or its impact. He remains aloof, inviolate. He bears no responsibility for his actions, since he is 'Wahy' or 'inspired'. This is hard to accept, especially in the light of the obvious earthly circumstances he is speaking into.

These incidents must and should be brought gently in a questioning format to Muslims, either to sow seeds of doubt to bear fruit in later years, or to stop wild accusations against the Christian community, to allow a more reasoned study of the gospels to take place. Whilst unrestricted and irrational allegiance holds the mind of the Muslim he is in no mood to consider the person of Christ.

This concrete involvement of Muhammad in worldly affairs is often given as a proof of his superiority over Christ, who never involved himself with men's lives but remained unmarried, apart from war, rule and political involvement. Hyperbole is a trait one comes across in most discussions with Muslims. One must not overreact when obviously outrageous claims are made. Egypt's Nasser was being sorely pushed by the Israeli army and King Hussein of Jordan called to ask if he needed help. No, was his reply, we are pushing them into the sea!! These over-optimistic statements are cultural accretions that Muslims pick up from the Qur'anic spirit. They can be answered with a smile and a sensitively couched question which leads to light in the mind of the deceived.

In many ways Shariati parallels Marx. His is a struggle to awaken the masses, shake the clerics out of their lethargy and deliver them from the opiate of the people by bringing struggle into religion. He clashed with his fellow clerics who he felt had surrendered to political pressure from the Shah's regime using 'takiyya' (hiding the faith in their heart) as an excuse for a quiet life; to run to 'takiyya' was to be a traitor to the greater good. His was a Marxist interpretation of Islam - again an Islamic vision in response to external stimuli.

In overtones of the Christian truth of life through death, Shariati sees man discovering his wealth when he perceives his poverty; when he feels his humility, he finds his pride and when surrendered to God he can rise against any power. There is a paradox deep within Christianity and in this sense Shariati is to discover (or appropriate) fresh ideas to reinvestigate and aid in interpreting Islam. Is this one example of the Christianisation that we spoke of above? Some active discovery of the great eternal truth in common grace that is for all men to buy as the pearl of great price? Has Shariati discovered the Spirit of New Testament and Christ's church? *Shirk*, associating something with God, is the antithesis of *tawhid*, God's transcendence from man and creation. Hijrah, Muhammad's flight from Mecca in 622 AD, is the emergence of the masses discovering their power and calling, as Marx called the workers of the world to unite and fulfil their destiny. The oneness of God (tawhid) is seen by him not as a number but an issue of the sovereignty of God; it is not a statement, but an enterprise of activity, subduing powers and principalities in opposition to God. He has discovered a paradox which most Muslims, influenced by Aristotle, vigorously deny exists; human reason and rationality are their master.

Kamil Hussein of Cairo

One who recognised and accommodated his thinking to the then growing all-pervasiveness of western culture was Kamil Hussein of Cairo. He studied medicine in France and England, where he came across the rationalism and humanism of Auguste Comte. Comte propounded that there was an evolution from superstition in primitive man leading to metaphysical ideas and then to scientific positivism. For Kamil, who was deeply Muslim, a fusion of his own and Comte's ideas developed an interesting interpretation of Islam.

Europe went through World Wars I and II and this carnage profoundly affected Kamil's view of the futility of war. He became deeply committed to a search for peace. He was committed to a scientific solution for the ills of the world. Politics were foreign to him. His solution diagnosed society and prescribed cures as a surgeon. His interests lay in 5 areas:

1) The nature of faith.

2) His own attitude to the Qur'an as a Revelation.

3) His estimate of Institutional Religion.

4) Inter-faith relations.

5) Pacifism, Peace and War Studies.

In all these he was eager for debate in a search of an answer. Unlike Fazlur Rahman, he does not see an obligation of awe of God coming from a command from God. Kamil felt that to be human was to have a basic awareness of the majesty of God. As a scientist, he placed this in the psyche of man and therefore it was observable and quantifiable. Just as the heart has a pulse to drive it, he argued, so man has a conscience; the pulse needs to be regulated and so also religion regulates man's conscience. Medicinal analogies are employed to give understanding of the ills of man and society and thus all religions have a part to play. His is a religion by observation and might appear not to need *wahy*, inspiration, and *tafsir*, commentary. All religious truth is personal and existential. *Wahy* and *tafsir* help people to express their faith. He therefore internalises Islam and rejects the harsher militancy of the fundamentalist. One could say there is an eclecticism in his approach, since Buddhism seems to be resembled in his preoccupation with personal soul life. He seems to have accepted the crucifixion contrary to Qur'anic and Islamic belief, calling it the 'darkest day in history' in his book 'City of Wrong'. The work is in fact a book of criticism of Islam. He, before all others, deals with the experience of the cross and thus relates to Christians. Can this be part or a development of his interest in suffering and pacifism, an understanding of the role in society of suffering by the innocent imposed by institutions unable to accommodate purity and innocence?

In all, Kamil is fascinated by the devotion and admiration Christ inspires almost in direct opposition to that of Muhammad. Islam provides a structure or religious framework for devotion but Christ is the empowerer of the heart. Kamil rejects the uniqueness of any religion and so tries to de-fanaticise religion. His existential approach to religion mixed with a loyalty to a mother religion, Islam, and a contact with other faiths leads him to try to synthesise all of them. Ecumenism for him is a means to discover the best for personal growth in all of them. He is honest enough to recognise the Islamic doctrine of the uncreatedness of the Qur'an as being comparable with the eternal logos of Christianity. After 1400 years a Muslim comes to see yet another borrowing by Islam from another source. As the virgin Mary gives birth to the logos, so the Arabic language gives the Qur'an.

The idea of the 'Createdness' or 'Uncreatedness' of the Qur'an has been a major source of conflict in the Islamic Umma down through the centuries. Remembering the sin of *shirk*, it is possible to argue that, if the Qur'an and God have always existed, then you have associated something with God and thus committed the sin of *shirk*. Again, as a result of being in contact with Christians, particularly in Damascus in the 9th century, Muslims argued that, as Christians believed in the eternal Word of God, so also their book should be eternal. Thus they fall into a pit they cannot climb out of. Logic and human reasoning cannot help them. Ultimately Kamil descended into despair as World War II progressed, which is the sure end of man's wisdom, which the writer of Ecclesiastes showed us many years ago, Vanity of Vanities.

CHAPTER 8
Moving on:
Hindrances to Global Evangelism

The world is in crisis. Millions of people wait and search and hope that they can find God. Many are trapped in demonic or oppressive systems and yet we Christians say we have the truth. If we do have it, surely there needs to be a life lived in the light of that reality. There are subtle hindrances to making the gospel both available and understandable to men and women of other cultures than our own. Here are just a few of them.

1) Management techniques as opposed to anointed and visionary leaders. In the secular world there has been a lot of emphasis on the management of time, down-sizing, management by objectives etc. These ideas have also infiltrated the church and church structures, many times to our advantage, but they can kill. God raises up men and women of vision and ability. It is He who gives to those servants gifts and skills that are to be used in the building up of the saints and the expansion of His kingdom. At times their spiritual drives run counter to perceived human wisdom and management principles. This is because He prompts men and women to prepare them for future events that management techniques cannot foresee. What seems foolishness to men is actually the wisdom of God. In missions there has been a greater emphasis on goal setting and the targeting of key people etc. Actually targets are used to shoot at and this reflects an attitudinal problem that missions have - that of seeing not people but merely objects to achieve their own goals. A leader with a vision from God will not be stopped but there may be some hard times, as office managers cannot see what the future is in the same way as the visionary can. Management tools are employed and rules implemented instead of relying on prayerful guidance of the Holy Spirit. This can easily dry up a ministry. It can destroy flexibility and sensitive relevance. Visionaries need manag-

ers but the manager must not choke the vision. You can have a well oiled organisation, but with no drive, passion or sense of calling it will not last long as an effective ministry in God's hands.

2) There are many valid and useful things that we can do in the life of the local church. However, it is necessary also to keep in perspective the need to balance our ongoing needs locally with the real state of the world in which we live. Would it not be better to weigh the pros and cons of holidays in various places against the more effective use of funds that could be given to keep ministries in front-line evangelism? Do we really need the very latest building or equipment in our churches? In isolation we can ignore the desperate needs of the battlefields both at home and overseas. Our own church has set up a building fund and 10% of it will be used for missions. This is a balanced approach towards the needs at home and the recognition of the wider world in which we are to serve.

3) Parochial vision as opposed to global thinking. Effective church leaders have the ability to see the greater picture. Too many react on impulse to something that presents itself on their breakfast tray. Too little global thinking and strategising goes on in the Christian Church. Muslims, Hindus, JW's and the cults are driven by a desire to rule the world; they have a plan. Can we not at least pray for the world in a strategic way and resist ungodly spirits that seek to keep man captive to unbelief and away from the message of the liberating power of the gospel?

4) The paternalism of sending and giving churches. The balance of the need for accountability and trust. Can we support these new emerging churches without tying them up in knots with conditions? I know one very valid ministry where 15 or so nationals were doing a good work amongst Muslims. A missionary passing through saw their absolute poverty and need for food and funds for their families, but insisted on giving them money only for literature. There is real misunderstanding and potential for conflict here, as western churches and agencies insist on a high degree of accountability for funds given. This is often interpreted by those receiving the money as being a lack of trust and an attempt to control. The danger, of course, is that money can have a corrupting influence and is open to misuse. Each side needs to understand the other's position and needs and adapt to those realities.

5) 'Faddism'. Many churches cannot be trusted to follow through with the commitments they make. Long term commitments are not part of the western culture and unfortunately this attitude has influenced the church; it has affected church loyalty, family life and missions involvement. The competitive nature of churches forces them to seek to have the very latest speaker or music or ministry in their programmes. A commitment given one year may well be abandoned as the church seeks to 'jump on the band wagon' of the latest fashion in ministry. One church I know made a commitment to helping to produce a Kurdish New Testament, but abandoned its promises when a boat ministry became the subject of the following year's missions conference.

6) Material comfort. Money spent on ice creams whilst children die for want of an injection, new cars, expensive holidays, all of us can think of the waste that goes on in our own lives and within our churches. May God give us grace to repent and return to a simple lifestyle for the sake of the rest of the world. Often our spending is linked to a sense of boredom and a disturbed spirit. This wasteful spending is often a means of finding an outlet to our psychological needs.

7) There is a growing trend in networking. No doubt these networks have brought great blessing but I have a suspicion that these conferences are an expensive foggy mist where nobody actually ends up doing anything that they would not have done anyway. In the end those with a calling and clear vision will move ahead despite what the rest of us say. Once again, the culture of the world, this time computer technology, sets the trend in the church and missions in this approach.

8) Ivory tower thinking in Academia. It is so easy to fall into the trap of being a Christian academician and not relate to the church's task of evangelism. The people who are confronting Islam in its new confidence, fuelled by Ahmad Deedat videos, are the young students who are least prepared for the questions they raise. We have some very fine academics, but unfortunately some remain isolated from the battlefield and cut and thrust of the debate concerning the person and work of Jesus Christ. We need Christian academics, people who put their minds to the service of the Church, but this must be allied to the call of the church and its obligations

to take the gospel to every creature. Academic study must be made relevant to the issues the church is facing and study in involvement with ministry will make this balance occur.

Western missionaries do have a unique role to play in this next phase of world evangelism; they are a major source of funding for overseas workers, a great source of skills such as researchers, technologists and administrators and a good source of inspiration and encouragement to others, and they have useful role in itinerant ministry. They must be ready, however, to be servants to these newly emerging churches. They must also come as learners. There is a wealth of insight and personal skills that they bring to western missions.

Witnessing to Muslims

The ignorance of Muslims concerning Christian belief is exceeded only by the ignorance of Christians concerning Islamic belief. Muslims believe that, because Muhammad said the Qur'an was the Word of God when it talks about what Christians believe, it must be true and correct. Nothing could be further from the truth.

The only proof ever given that the Qur'an is true is that Muhammad said it was. The only proof that Muhammad came from God is that the Qur'an says he did, QED? Thus by circular reasoning and being in a closed system they cannot entertain any other proposition.

If you are able to highlight errors in the Qur'an, you can discount the Qur'an as the basis for truth and revelation. This is because Muslims state that the book came down from heaven intact and perfect. The smallest mistake in the Qur'an renders the entire holy book to be null and void because of this perfect status given to it by Muslims. In fact, the most effective literature in the Victorian period was that which went to the heart of the matter, critically analysing the Qur'an's integrity. Books such as 'Balance of Truth' (Pfander), 'Historical Development of the Qur'an' (Sell) and 'How the Qur'an was compiled' (Kader). Others followed, written by authors like Wansbrugh, Jeffrey, Juynboll, Schacht and, in later years, Gilchrist. Even today modern Islamic scholars like Abd al Aziz Fahmi claim that the Uthmanic text is absurd. This gives us great ground for prayer that cracks might further develop in their thinking and that the doubts which arise will lead to a deeper inquiry into the nature of God and faith in Jesus Christ.

These are all books that have borne fruit. The greatest enemy of Islam is in fact modern western education. This is because it is a system based upon the critical examination of evidence. It was Shabbir Akhtar in the September 15th 1995 issue of The Times Educational Supplement that said "Islam says nothing; it is Muslims who say many things".

How do we know that Guy Fawkes ever lived, that Nelson won the battle of Trafalgar or that Paul Revere rode a horse? It is through critical, objective analysis of the evidence. Scientific discovery, artistic development, and all knowledge is achieved by questioning and critiquing what we have, to avoid deception.

The Islamic world is trying to modernise through the fruits of modern technology (without also taking on the philosophy of the West). They have sought to imitate western education and graft it on to an Islamic philosophical root, thus producing critics in Egypt, Morocco, Bangladesh and the other nations of Islam. Only fear holds this mediaeval society together and the rejection of Islamic ideologies is growing. This once great and developed civilisation does not want to be seen to have been left behind by superior forces and so a form of schizophrenia is developing. They need to adopt new technologies but it must be Islamicised. This in fact was also the way that Islam grew to be a great civilisation, by usurping the Persian and Byzantine empires and laying their system on top of the one already present. The 'golden era' of Islam is actually a myth. There was a steady decline of the societies under the Byzantines, which simply accelerated under the Muslims. Tax returns from the earliest periods show a steady decline in the lands that they took over. Islam did not produce a great golden age by itself but rather rode to the conclusion of one already started, wasting resources and crushing the human spirit in the process.

One of the mistakes that many Christians make is to compare Muhammad with Christ. Such a comparison is not possible. For the Muslim, Muhammad is only a prophet (Nabi), a warner (mundhir) and messenger (rasul). He did not change, add to or affect the Qur'an in any way, so they believe. This is, of course, not true. For example, at one time he saw his adopted son Zaid's wife bathing and desired her as David did Bathsheba. Since it was not possible under ancient Arab custom to marry your son's wife, he could not have her. Fortunately for Muhammad, a revelation came saying that under Islam there is no adoption. Zaid was free to divorce his wife and allow Muhammad to marry her.

In fact what Muslims have on earth is said to be a copy of what exists in heaven. The word of God for the Christian is in fact not the Bible but Christ (John 1¹). Of course, in one sense we believe that the Bible is the word of God, but that is only a shadow of a greater truth: that the word became flesh and dwelt amongst us. This is a mystery, but, if God is God, surely we must expect to find a mystery; otherwise, if He is fully understood, neither should we need a revelation nor would He be a God greater than man. We ought then to compare Christ with the Qur'an (if Christ is to be compared at all) and the four gospels only describe and present the Word of God in Christ. In Islam there must be four witnesses to some events. Thus we could say that the four gospels fulfil the Islamic requirement for evidence concerning Christ. They are all witnesses of the same event from different perspectives. Matthew describes the life of Christ to Jewish people, Mark does the same thing for the Romans, Luke talks in terms that Greeks can understand and John portrays Jesus for who He is rather than what He did.

The Qur'an was found to be extremely limited in its ability to provide legal rulings for the new Islamic empires of Syria and Persia and Egypt. To compensate, there arose a body of verbal tradition called Hadith, which was eventually written down. This occurred around 850 AD and covers some 600,000 supposed sayings. Schacht claims that none of them is actually true, but that they were all invented in order to allow Muslims to incorporate the Jewish, Roman and Christian laws into Islam by saying that Muhammad had actually taught concerning these things anyway. Bukhari, who is a collector of the Hadith himself, claims that only 7397 out of the 600,000 are actually true, in that the others did not actually take place. One Arab scholar, Ibn Abu Dawned in his book 'Kitts al Masahif' says that there were several thousand variants of the Qur'an in those early years. With the lack of credibility of support texts like the Hadith and the many variants of the Qur'an, there is no way that the Qur'an itself can stand up in any court of law. It has to be defended in another way. That way is threefold:

Firstly, to criticise other holy books first and turn the attention away from the Qur'an. Secondly, never to allow criticism of the Qur'an or Hadith within educational establishments or media (if it occurs, then to try vigorously to refute the allegations). Finally, to threaten with death anybody who discounts the originator of the Qur'an, Muhammad, or his family. Salmon Rushdie's exposure of Islam was in this vein.

There arises thus the oppression of any dissidents amongst them. For a Muslim, Islam is the pearl of all religions, the greatest, and Muhammad is the reason why God created the Universe. It is seen as the most perfect religion and is not like Judaism, which is a religion of the law, or Christianity, which teaches people to turn the other cheek (and therefore is not a practical religion). It is an everyday man's sort of religion. A Muslim on pilgrimage can take a wife for a weekend or even a night as long as he recites the appropriate formula, marrying her and divorcing her the next day. It allows account for man's (not woman's) physical need!

Some of you may be called to speak to a group of Christians about issues that will attract a Muslim audience. Or you may be asked to share with a Muslim audience either in a College or University setting, possibly in an interfaith meeting or other such event. You may well be faced with a barrage of questions to which the questioners do not really want an answer but they simply want to "roll you over" by the sheer weight of the volume of questions.

Once I was asked to speak at a church in Cardiff, South Wales, on the subject of Islam, as they had a Muslim community within their parish. What I did not know was that some dear unsuspecting deacon had advertised the meeting in the local newspaper. The result was that a man turned up asking if he and friends from the mosque could attend. I really do not like Muslims in my meetings, which are designed for Christians, since one cannot speak effectively to both groups. I therefore declined. However they were insistent and finally I relented with the proviso that the Friday night meeting would be for a mixed group and the Saturday would be for Christians only.

On the Friday night I showed slides and spoke about the history of Islam, finishing by inviting questions from the audience. One Muslim stood up immediately and asked three completely unrelated apologetical questions, not to me, but to the Christian audience who were meekly waiting. After he had asked his questions another Muslim stood wanting to ask something as well. You will find all Muslims will want to be seen to be defending Islam and to be seen to be attacking Christianity. Knowing the technique, I stopped the proceedings and told the audience that the first man had asked an important question: "Why were there four gospels when only one Qur'an was required?". This is a beautiful question to use to explain many aspects of the gospel story and, of course, the gospel itself. At the end of my reply another man stood to ask his question, but I stood on my ground and told him to sit down and not to be so rude, because the first man had not had his second question answered. Thus the event was controlled and used to share the gospel.[1]

On another occasion a group of Muslims came into a church in north London where I was teaching. They, of course, objected to the historical view of Islamic development and wanted to claim that it grew because God was with them. They went on to speak highly of the teaching of Islam. Wanting to short-circuit the debate, I asked them for an example of where pure Islam had ever been practised, at any time, in any place in the world. There was silence as they quickly scrolled through the many catastrophic events in Islamic history and finally they said that it was pure at the time of Muhammad and the four Rasidun, rightly-guided Caliphs, Abu Bakr, Omar, Uthman and Ali. They seemed to have forgotten that Muhammad had assassinated men in Mecca who had written satirical poetry about him and that Omar, Uthman and Ali had all been assassinated by members of the Islamic body politic and only Abu Bakr had died naturally as an old man, two years after his appointment as successor to Muhammad.

---

[1] The reason why Anis Shoresh lost in his debate with Ahmad Deedut and Josh Mc Dowell won against him was that Josh and Ahmad are debaters, but Anis is a preacher not a debater.

However, can Christians claim any more? No, of course, not. Church history is full of conflict and greed. But I am a Christian, not because I am perfect or because Christianity produces a perfect political system (despite what the Moral Majority would like to claim), but because I am forgiven. Only forgiveness distinguishes Christianity, in the broader sense of the word, from Islam. Only the crucified sacrifice of Himself shows what God is really like: not the harsh lawgiver, not the judge and executioner of men, not the distant 'Malik' or owner of men's souls, not the one who changes his mind at a whim and a fancy, but one who also knows suffering. One time I called on a friend in Sheffield to have tea with him. By the time I had arrived he had telephoned an Iranian contact, who agreed to come over and cook an Iranian meal for me (only Iranians know how to cook rice). After the meal we read Isaiah 53 and the man then wept. He saw that the Christ we followed had suffered like a man also. He had fled the Iranian revolution and had lost his family to the four winds. He needed a God who knew how he felt - a God who had suffered.

In the west our education and career moves are all based upon competition and being better than others. In God's world the 'spoils' go to the weak, the humble and the oppressed. God blesses and gives the increase and too many times we feel that the most educated will actually be the most successful in missions. It has been proved over and over again that the man or woman that God uses is he or she who will not take the glory and who gives the honour to God. If you feel weak in the face of this task, be encouraged; God may have you just where he can begin to use you.

CHAPTER 9
Discipling and Church Planting

The 'in' word today is 'Church Planting'. If you are not Church Planting you really are seen to be a second class missionary. Many missions which were doing a very valuable job in reaching men and women have been forced to change their policies and strategies in order to accommodate the new fad that has arisen, mainly from the USA. There is a great danger that this emphasis on church planting will undermine the long-term need to disciple men and women effectively out of an Islamic culture into a biblical spirituality.

Often workers are sent to do Church Planting work without experience or proper training of Church Planting, having never done it even within their own culture. Such is the state of the western Church. Theory is divorced from reality. We have become information kiosks, as Packer describes us, rather than imparters of life and reality. Leaders send troops into battle, having never been on the field themselves.

On reflection, however, it would be difficult to find a biblical text that would support this emphasis. In all four gospels there is no direct reference to Church Planting per se at all. Christ calls believers to work and stay together and gives them structures by which they remember Him. The formation of a loving community is a better description of the process of the gospel. Paul certainly does not refer to Church Planting as a command and it seems to me that Church Planting is a natural outgrowth of an even more important principle. With the over-emphasis of the Church Planting mode there has been a loss of emphasis on the more important principle that Jesus used in training His disciples and that they and Paul later implemented. Even Paul was discipled by Barnabas. The discipling of new converts is essential for growth to take place. Indeed in our present Church situation in Britain it seems that even the older converts are themselves in desperate need of discipling. Thankfully, this lack of emphasis is being restored by many of the new growing Churches, as found in Brazil, Korea and Singapore. Indeed it can be argued that this different emphasis actually stems from a current cultural climate.

In the USA many are attending church. It is relatively easy to gather a group of people together and start a new church or denomination. All you need to do is pick a city, target a semi-affluent community and you can have your church. Thus planting new churches by moving out of the inner city and ghetto will guarantee success. This ease fills people with delight and is seen to be the panacea for all the world's troubles. Simply go out and do the same as has been done in the local scene there in the USA. After all, it's the same message and the same Lord, they reason.

In Brazil much of their Church growth came about along with the animistic accretions of Brazilian culture. The need was not to start new Churches but to 'detoxify' those who were coming into the Church. Thus they have developed a discipling programme. Each person in the Church is either being taught or is teaching and in many cases doing both. Thus they learn and teach, teach and learn. The material thus taught becomes part of their life and in-depth personal maturity takes place. The material is an agent for change and not an end in itself. Commentaries are not for the grasping of the text but a tool to understand the text and its message, significant to their lives.

Rev. Willi Still in Aberdeen has little theological training, but is personally responsible for much of the growth in evangelicalism in the Church of Scotland. He hand-picked and trained younger men. The method changes to suit the culture but the principle stands in whatever culture you choose.

In theory the Anglican system of a curacy or the earlier Brethren model of training young men in the scriptures should hold, but people get tired. Few of us are willing to open up our lives and live a transparent life so that the younger ones in the Lord see us in all our weaknesses and yet also see "Christ in us, the hope of glory". It is not our success and strengths that reveal Christ, but the weakness and pain that we go through that show His life in us. Our power and strength often discourage new believers, because they cannot imagine that they could ever be like us. However, when we confess our weaknesses and show our vulnerability, they can relate to that and draw inspiration and encouragement. Thus the method falls down due to human tiredness or lack of vision as to the potential of the method. Discipling others requires spiritual, emotional and psychological vitality. However the alternative is even worse; decay, disintegration, legalism and traditionalism take the place of a living school of maturing new members.

In Africa it would be very difficult to find any theological institution that prepared a student for ministry within an African context. Most of their seminaries or theological centres have been set up by westerners, with a western curriculum that parrots western institutions and western world views. This, of course, leads to producing African leaders that relate very well to overseas education but not to the local scene, and so many leave for the West. Jesus' method would be far more relevant to Africa and Asia and, of course, to the Islamic world. What a revolution would take place if Pastors and elders actually trained young men and women on a person to person basis and were in fact a confirmation of their own ministry!

What I have tried to do is to see the potential in each person and then move them into positions where they can be exposed and be responsible for their actions and thus grow in their ministry. This trust is open to abuse but generally allows that person to grow and develop. I have had many young men say to me that I was the first person who really trusted them. Too many times leaders are afraid to allow people to make mistakes that are the very source of growth and gaining relevant experience.

In considering the Islamic world, the need is for the in-depth discipling of men and women so that they can then go on to train and disciple others. One to one training stands as the key issue in the growth of the Church in the Muslim world today. The details change, but the principle is the same. It is done on a one to one basis. It, of course, fits more naturally also into the cultural pattern that one finds in Islamic lands.

Often Islamic education has been carried out by a Sheikh moving about from city to city or even country to country, having an expertise to share. He is often supported by his disciples by their bringing a chicken or food to pay for their room and board, as it were. In some cases the Sheikh supplies the food. This is because he has become famous and has been given gifts of land or property from which he can support those who come to place themselves under his feet (and by implication under his authority). Sometimes he owns many villages and there is much wealth in his hands. This is true in Kurdistan. However this wealth is not for his own personal gratification. It has been given to him to administer to take care of his 'children', the community.

This model of the Sheikh or "Ustad" and student or "Shagird" is more like an open-ended apprenticeship. The student moves on only when the Sheikh is satisfied that he has actually learned what was needed to be learned. This is not based upon an examination system but by observation of his behaviour. Jesus in fact was the Master teacher and chose to do this. He sent out the 70 to gain experience and see what powers they did have. Then, of course, there is the launching of the church at Pentecost, where the church learned by doing. The Lord never had a classroom, a curriculum or an examination system, but He taught very effectively. This intensification of personal relationships inculcating a teachable spirit and designing an atmosphere where people can grow and reflect the teacher's works and words is a powerful model.

But what areas will need to be addressed in a convert's life? If we go back to 'Insan al Kamil', we see that the person of Muhammad stands as a strong, overpowering personality that binds thinking, actions, emotions, loyalties and feelings. This desire to have a model must be re-focused upon Christ and the pristine character of Jesus Christ must be reproduced in the believer through the Holy Spirit in accordance with the word of God. The convert must become intoxicated with the gospels. Then there are certain character faults that have to be changed. Sex and the sexual activities found in the Hadiths are very strong. These must be cleansed with a proper view of God's creative gifts. This introduces us to the attitude towards women and females and the need to protect, cherish and listen to them as equals. This may be done without destroying the unique relationship and different roles that men and women share in the structure of the family and society. To understand this better, it would be good to read the critiques emerging now from the Islamic world, by writers like Sadawi, Mernissi and even Sasson in her books 'Princess' and 'Daughters of Arabia'. Some of these books are not academic works, but they are a cry for help from a large part of society that is stifled and oppressed by traditions that no longer have any meaning. These traditions have been used by men to control, use and exploit to their own advantage fellow human beings.

In Shia Islam a man is allowed, under the authority of an Islamic formula, to marry a woman for a night if need be, if he is away from his own wife on a pilgrimage or a business trip. The Iranian revolution broke out as the Shah's wife destroyed the "Muta" marriage houses around the tomb of the Imam Reza in Mashad. Such was the attraction of this privilege accorded to men. Victory over this area of thought life is crucial, otherwise it can lie like a time bomb ready to go off at a time designed to cause maximum damage.

Trust and truth must be built. A deeper understanding of absolute truth and the reliability of the scriptures must be a priority. The model that scripture is for guidance is already strong for a Muslim, but when conversion takes place this often leads to a legalism and infighting with other converts. This is because they see the Bible as giving an absolute answer in areas that it actually leaves open to individual conscience. The Bible's absolutism actually is in moral and spiritual areas and not in the eating of meat, holding of festivals or keeping of traditions. The teacher must be clear himself about this issue. I have to say this because the Church in the West is so weak that traditions are held as being God given and thus even potential disciplers need setting free. How often have a young person's new ideas been turned down by elders who have said that they have done such and such before and see no need for change.

Takiyya is a legal means of staying alive if your life is threatened. You are allowed to 'hide' your faith as long as you remain a Muslim in your heart. This, of course, then is used to justify all sorts of lying and is the thin edge of the wedge for telling lies. Added to this is the strong emotion of saving face and not being caught out. It builds a strong incentive to lie in the face of a difficult situation. Guilt, and ultimately a rejection of the Christian faith, quickly ensues. Leadership must be exercised on a consultative basis rather than the western authoritative style of decision making. Dr. Elizabeth Jones has an excellent article on cultural differences, eastern and western style. In it she points out the four dimensions of culture that Hofstede identified in his book 'Cultures and Organizations-Software of the Mind' (McGraw Hill 1992, Europe). Thus through the religious teaching excuses are given for telling and living a lie.

Tribalism is rampant in today's world. As modern communications shrink our world, we feel threatened by losing our identity as people. This is leading to a re-emphasis on our distinctives and therefore our difference from others. Sectarian, cultural, linguistic and religious differences are highlighted and our own group is elevated to being "the best" and any others denigrated as being inferior. Becoming a Christian means that we appreciate the variety of humankind and glory in the fact that God has allowed or given us the freedom to be different. We need to emphasise that our differences should not put down others but should cause us to be humbled and become teachable. The differences should lead us to learn about the inadequacies of our own culture and draw from and learn from others. Recently I was teaching in Prague and wanted to bring out the Arab imperialism of Islam over other peoples. I led the enquiry by asking the students which language was the most beautiful. To a man (and woman) they all exclaimed that Czech was the most beautiful, of course. Then they realised what they had said and burst out laughing. I then seriously told them that they were wrong and that they had got the answer wrong. Again the question was put to them and they searched for the right answer. Again laughter when I told them that English was the most beautiful. Thus we both had committed the sin of ethnocentrism. Having lived under communism and Russian imperialism, they realised that Communism had been a vehicle for cultural domination. Thus, when a Muslim is told that Arabic is the language of heaven and that he must pray, read the works of God and declare his faith in Arabic, he is being dominated by another culture. God never does that. He sets us free to express ourselves and to be beautiful people in our own terms.

The ultimate discipler is the Holy Spirit. Jesus in John's gospel says that He will be with you and in you (John 16 v 13). He is to conform us to the image of the Lord Jesus Christ (Rom. 8 v 29). He is to teach us all things (John 14 v 25). These and many other verses are to help us understand that in the final analysis it is He, the Spirit of truth, that guides, leads, empowers and equips the new believer. Just this year I was with an Afghan believer who was such an example of a man of God. He had come to know Christ through the ministry of our leader in India. I wanted to know how he had been able to build his life around Christ and be free from the life he had led before. Over and over again he said that the Lord had shown him that this and that were wrong. As he learned of Christ's love for him, he grew in love and in turn loved his family and wife. His wife saw this new man and was attracted to Christ herself, when she saw Him in her husband. They now have a lovely family atmosphere where there is no rivalry or domination of one over the other, but they have all the aspects that one would think a Muslim would have to be taught as he grows in Christ. We can trust Him to conform His children to the image of His dear Son.

CHAPTER 10

Church Planting Methods Observed

From my observations there have been eight basic ways that God has used to start His work in Muslim lands. This has not yet led to significant church planting, although seminal groups are there, meeting in homes and studying the Word of God;

1) *The Apostolic method.*
2) *The Team method, both long and short-term.*
3) *Crisis method.*
4) *Institutional method.*
5) *Mass media.*
6) *International church method.*
7) *Through signs and wonders.*
8) *The incarnational method.*

The Apostolic Method

We all admire the apostles. In some way we see the apostles as those who suffered for the gospel and line up with the men of faith in Hebrews chapter 11. Paul probably exemplifies the apostles' life style and we know that he was beaten and imprisoned and suffered abuse for the sake of taking the gospel to lands which did not know of Christ. This is what I mean by the "Apostolic" method.

As I look back over my experiences in the Muslim world, I see certain ways in which the church has been planted. The first way is what I would call the Apostolic Way. I suppose every Bible School student wants to be like the apostle Peter or Paul but let's remember that the apostolic way was also the suffering way. A friend of mine was driving through Turkey to go to Afghanistan. On giving out some tracts in Erzurum in Eastern Turkey they were arrested and imprisoned for a month. On their release they went off to Afghanistan. Ten years later they were coming back through

Erzurum and found a church there. On asking how the church was
started they were told a story by some men. As small boys they used
to go to the prison and sit on the wall. One time they had heard men
singing in the prison and they were singing about Jesus. They
wondered at people being so happy whilst imprisoned, so they
decided to get a Bible and find out more about this Jesus. Thirty of
them came to Christ and they started meeting together to study the
Bible; in effect a new church had been planted in Turkey! God can
use for good what we believe to be a bad experience.

You could not plan for that event, but you can try to be sensitive to what God is telling you and be sure you are in the right place
at the right time each day of the year. Even so, if you are not, is God
too small to weave it into His plan for good? Did He not know
beforehand anyway?

The Team Method

Another way that I have seen churches planted is through short-
term summer teams. I believe in short-term missions and in long-
term missions also. WIN has an "adopt a province" programme.
There are 67 provinces in Turkey. The idea is for a church or Bible
school or family to adopt one province all through the year to pray
and study about the adopted province, and then in the summer to
visit for 3 weeks. Take 10 New Testaments each, but don't do any
evangelism; just enjoy the people. Drink tea, play football, go
swimming, go fishing with them. The Turkish people are very
hospitable and will say "Come and eat my food, come to my house,
come to my sister's wedding". When they have done something for
you, you have to return the favour. So you give them a gift, a New
Testament. In that way it is not evangelism but it is a natural way
of sharing the word of God whilst being culturally sensitive. To
refuse a gift from a guest would be unthinkable.

We have a family in the south of England that has adopted a
province. Every summer they go back to the same province and
visit the people who have received New Testaments. They talk to
them, they pray with them, and already Muslims have been baptised.
There has not been any foreigner to control them. There has not
been the problem of the security police, and therefore there has
been friendship established over a long period of time. So gradually

through short-term teams churches are being planted and I would like to encourage you to go this summer to one of these areas. Take your Pastor with you and make your missions programme in your church realistic. One of the ladies that goes out to this area is 74 years old. Both of her hips have been replaced with plastic. Nearly everybody in your church can be involved in church planting in the Muslim world, as part of this ongoing programme of prayer and study, of visits and vitally of re-visits. A wide age range of people can go in a group, making it easier to talk to a wider range of people abroad.

It would be a benefit to look at the actual process of church planting. Often we send teams of western missionaries who will witness to the local people, resulting in one or two converts who come together. Let us say you have a team of westerners consisting of 10 people and you see 4 or 5 converts come. When these people meet, it is the western culture that dominates. Even in their own country you are extracting the local Christians out of their culture thus westernising them. In turn this often leads to resentment and conflict amongst the non-Christian locals. Team work often leads to being a psychological crutch for people away from their own culture. They in fact never become cross-cultural people, because they continue to live in a western team atmosphere.

As I look at the Arab world, I find that it is mainly through Palestinian, Jordanian and Egyptian Christians that church growth has occurred. What has happened? The western Christians have been used to disciple a few local Christians; it is these Palestinians that are at the cutting edge of Muslim work. By trying to form the church around ourselves we actually import a foreign form of Christianity. If we deliberately step back and allow local people to lead, they will find their own level of manifestation of church life within that culture. It may very well be different from what we would expect or desire but it will be indigenous. One dear friend was a Palestinian who worked in a Middle Eastern country. He knew the language, understood the culture and loved the people. It was in his professional capacity that he was able to meet many high ranking people and in the process gently explained the gospel. The last time I met him he was discipling a Sheikh and his four wives! Peter Cotterell of London Bible College tells the story of his experience in Ethiopia where Muslims had come to know the Lord and they had four wives. What were the missionaries to teach the new converts? They refused to give a pat answer and taught the new believers to seek the Lord, search the scriptures and find their own God-given solutions. They did and it was not one that the missionaries would have dreamed of.

A variation of the team method is that developed by Lawrence Khong in Singapore. In this method cell groups are established and leaders identified has been shown to work very successfully in some Islamic lands and in the face of government and other pressures the cell group can survive. It does depend upon strong leadership but that very well suits the cultural mind set of the peoples we are working with.

If you go to Pakistan you will see English churches; they have bells and symbols all from the west. What is needed in Pakistan is Pakistani churches with Pakistani music, with Pakistani theology. There is a theology now coming from Africa. There is a theology coming from South America, as the Christians study theology and study the Bible.

The Crisis Method

In Indonesia there are 1 million Muslims who have come to Christ. Why did they come? Because there was a crisis, a political crisis, in the country and they had to be either a Christian or a Muslim (they could not be communist). Through this political chaos many people came into the church. We see the same thing in Iran: the church in Iran is growing. How? Through chaos. Look at China. The church is growing in China because there have been chaos and crises. A hundred years ago there was no church in Korea. Now over 25% of Korea is Christian. How did that happen? Because there was crisis. There were difficulties in the country. Wherever there is suffering, Christ is there. Where is the suffering today? Kurdistan, and Kurds are coming to Jesus because they have found that Islam has no answer, communism has no answer, materialism has no answer. Westernisation has no answer. They have temporary answers but that is it, and therefore, when we are thinking about church planting in the Muslim world, we should first of all concentrate on where the problems are and consider how we might help the people.

Many have come to know Christ through the practical help that churches and missions have given in times of great stress and trial. Famine, floods, war and other calamities have all played their part in destroying lives in these nations. When Christian agencies help and Muslim nations come in only to teach the law, the people see the difference. Many leprosariums have been staffed in these lands by Indian Christian nurses because they were not afraid to be contaminated by such a disease. Yes, it is possible that aid will produce "rice" Christians, that is those who convert for financial or material advantage, but to withhold help in these times of need would be sin to the Church of Jesus Christ.

The Institutional Method

Today we seem to be getting back to using institutions and that is where the church has also grown in the past, mainly through medical or educational work. The church in India, for example, was involved in hospitals and schools and the church has grown because of those institutions. Now maybe they do not have the fire of preaching on the streets, but they demonstrate the love of Christ. They meet what is called a 'felt need' and the Muslim people see that it is the Christians who are helping them and so they are saying "Why is it that Christians help us but Islam does not?" Look at Afghanistan, where there has been much, much suffering. Who are helping the Afghans? The Christians. Not the Muslim world, not Saudi Arabia, not Libya. Libya is giving them guns, but guns do not help when your children are dead. It is the Christians who are getting alongside them and suffering with the Muslim people. The danger is that institutional work is expensive and can create dependent churches by giving work to converts. It can also lead to a fear of witnessing in case those very institutions need to be protected from an oppressive government. It has been the church that has opened hospitals in these needy areas, even in the Gulf, where rulers have given land to missions to open such hospitals. This has not always been because of love for their own people, but because they want to have available medical care near their families.

Mass Media

The church is growing in the Muslim world through mass dissemi-
nation of the word of God. This can be through a variety of means
- Arabic radio programmes and literature for example (and so we
have organisations like OM, Every Home Crusade and the Bible
League, involved in the distribution of scriptures and books). We
need to see increased distribution of scriptures and we need to see
creative ways of distributing the word of God come about, for
example by using secular magazines to advertise Bible correspondence courses.

We have an Arabic-speaking team who have been working with
the Bible correspondence course in southern Spain. There are some
3300 people in Morocco who have written asking for a Bible correspondence course. They have not all received answers because
there are not enough Arabic speaking people to write the letters.
Why not? There is only one reason. Few have been released into
this work because of lack of finances. There are Christians in the
Lebanon and Egypt who have been to Bible School but do not have
the money to go to Morocco. We have an untapped resource which
is not being put to work. The church must wake up to financing the
Christians who are available but who do not have the money. You
could study Arabic all your life and you still would not know enough
to be able to answer the letters. It must be somebody from within
the Arab culture who does the Bible correspondence course work.
The westerners can do the technical things like radio and television
and run printing presses and organise translation work, but ultimately it has to be somebody from within the culture that reaches
these people.

International Church Method

The need for western expertise in education, construction and industry has opened the way for many foreigners from the West and
people from Korea and Singapore have been drawn to Muslim lands
to find work. Among these there have been believers: some of them
are there for the money, some for the sake of the gospel. Out of this
community churches have been born that use English, Korean and
German, for example, as their language of worship. Churches have
sprung up in Istanbul, Teheran, Riyadh and other such capitals.

They have attracted the interest of local people and some have been invited to the services by their foreign friends. The result has been a steady flow of converts sometimes eventually leading to an independent church being formed.

Signs and Wonders

Probably the most discussed and debated area in missions has been the emergence of an emphasis on the Holy Spirit, as expressed in the Charismatic movement. All I can do is to relate what I have seen and heard. The fact is that about eighty per cent of all Muslim converts have actually come to Christ through a dream or a miraculous healing. Indeed the Pentecostal movement has probably made the greatest inroad into Islam. This, I believe, is because they believe, understand and teach their people about the supernatural world in which we have our being. God is willing to meet people where they are. People in non-western societies live their lives by dreams and therefore He uses them to speak to them. However it is also easy to have dreams from another source. I have known Muslims who have been confirmed in their faith by having a dream of Muhammad. The Shah of Iran claimed that Hussein, Muhammad's son, came to him in a dream and told him to build a new Islamic society. That is not to discount dreams, but it presses us to seek spiritual answers and insights to the dream that is being shared. Dreams can come from several sources;

Firstly, from God: see Gen. 28[12], Jacob's dream at Bethel; Gen. 40[12], Joseph's interpretation of the butler's dream; Gen. 46[2], God speaks to Israel regarding Egypt. God guided His people through prophets to whom He gave a dream.

Secondly, from Satan and false prophets: Deut. 13[1-5]. We need to test all dreams to be sure they are from God.

Thirdly from a disturbed sub-conscious mind: guilt can play on a person's mind and be expressed through the sub-conscious.

Finally from some physical input, such as over-eating or an event of the day causing a physical reaction.

We can actually attribute dreams to Natural, True or False causes. Just as alternative forms of medicine are practised by people who have no access to modern or good medical help, so also alternative forms of guidance are looked for by people who lack an open revelation or a knowledge of the place of the Holy Spirit. Never has there been a time like today when people are running after occult practices for guidance and wisdom. Lost people are looking at horoscopes, taking to Tarot cards and seeking mediums for guidance.

Every day I ask and expect God to guide me. If I miss a bus I accept that He knows about it and can turn my missing the bus into good if I turn it over to Him. Similarly a man with no knowledge about God will turn to thoughts, to images of imagination and to outside influences to try to understand and interpret his daily experiences. In both the Old and New Testaments, dreams and visions were part and parcel of people's lives. God utilised them to guide His people. For Peter it was the way God used to bring him into a new understanding of God's plan for the Gentiles. Other examples can be found in the following passages:

• Gen. 37$^{2-11}$; Gen. 42^9: Joseph's dreams regarding his brothers.

• Daniel 2$^{1-49}$: Daniel's interpretation of Nebuchadnezzar's dreams.

• Acts 9$^{1-19}$: Saul on the Damascus road.

• Acts 10$^{9-16:}$ Peter's need to understand what was clean and unclean.

In church history Tertullian, St. Francis of Assisi, St. Anthony and Thomas of Aquinas all had dreams. So it is today. God is giving Muslims dreams about Himself and leading them to an interpreter of that dream in order to bring them to Christ. Some time ago I was in Chicago and was asked by a lady who taught English to a mixed group of Arabs; that is, Arabs from various countries. She asked me to come to their house and share with them. It is not a situation I like because you can't just sit down and run through a check list with Muslims for evangelism. You take time to be their friend first. However I was the 'expert' and so I went along. The result was that I ended up witnessing to the white American fiancée of one of the Egyptians there.

Listening to the conversation was a Tunisian who later came to Christ, all without my knowing about it. When he was a child he had seen a figure in his bedroom and had run to his parents afraid of the 'spirit'. That image stayed with him and there in a Chicago tenement building he recognised that it was Christ who had come to him as a boy.

On another occasion I was in the mountains of the Kabyle in Algeria. I gave a tract to an old man sitting on the ground in a market place. Looking at it quizzically he asked what it was. I told him to take it home to his grandson who would read it to him. It would tell him about God. His reply startled me. Some years ago he had seen in a dream a tall figure with white hair, glowing eyes and a sword coming out of his mouth. I read the passage in Revelation and he exclaimed "Yes, that's the man".[1]

The Incarnational Method

Actually this is not a method so much as an attitude that should permeate every other method. I include it as a method because we in the West tend to categorise everything, often losing sight of the moral qualities that must underpin all that we do. For example we might separate a teacher from his moral behaviour. He may be a pervert, but as long as he is a 'good' teacher he is allowed access to children and becomes an example to them. Slowly the western churches are waking up to the fact that a person's way of life is more important than their ability to debate, evangelise, sell literature, preach, heal or any other activity. Any area of hypocrisy will easily be exposed by sensitive Muslim spirits. For this reason many missions have eliminated divorcees from those qualified to be missionaries. Once a pattern of relational breakdown occurs, it is easier to allow for another under the pressure of cross cultural living.

Let me go through some questions you must address:

1) We must have a philosophy of church planting so that we have a clear picture in our minds first of all of what the problems are and how to go about them. To attain some of those goals it is necessary to take the new candidate through stages of growth in ministry. Are you going to go out and plant a western style of church? Are you going to start a Korean Presbyterian church in

---

[1] I am grateful to Richard Bailey who is the only person I know who has written a research paper on the place of dreams and visions in Muslim evangelism. It is well worth reading.

Saudi Arabia? What about Tashkent and Bukhara and Samarkand? Are we going to have Korean Presbyterian churches there? Or are we going to have a Turkic church? Now the people at your home church will not like it because they want you to reproduce a clone of their preferences. They give money supposing that you are going to reproduce something that they perceive to be a biblical model. After all, isn't our own church the genuine New Testament model?! You have got to have the wisdom to start something that is in context to the local environment. This means using local music and allowing spiritual growth to express local culture within the restraints of Christian expression.

2) You have to have some goals. Who is going to go? When are they going to go? How are you going to work? Where are you going to send those people? I would like to suggest that you send people first of all to a place where they are not going to be long-term. If you are planning to go to Afghanistan, then go and work in Turkey first; if you are going to North Africa, then go to Lebanon first. Begin to get some experience in your own life before you go to your target area. This is not to say that you should make mistakes in someone else's backyard, but rather that you go to any area of less intensity and greater pastoral oversight initially. Who is going to work with you? Do they have matching or conflicting gifts? David had Jonathan and Paul had Barnabas; each of us needs a faithful man who will believe in us and work with us in spite of the troubles and warfare that will come. You need someone whom you can trust and who will not treacherously turn on you when the going gets tough.

3) Then you need to do some research and a survey of the area. You need to get knowledge and personal experience of where you are going. So whilst you are living in Turkey go and visit Afghanistan. Gradually you begin to become aware of what the issues really are. Research and survey will help to get to know the people in depth. As you get to know them, they will reveal to you a way of communicating the gospel in appropriate forms.

4) Then there needs to be reinforcement: Islamics and other specialist training. The Ichthus church London has planted between thirty and forty churches in London and has now set up a training centre in Cyprus. You actually learn church planting by

doing it. Few missionaries have actually been involved in church planting before going to the field. This is all part of our academic arrogance. We assume because we are educated that we can actually do the work. Ichthus places you in church planting work in London, then you go to Cyprus and you learn all about the culture of the Middle East before you depart for your target country. I meet so many missionaries who never have studied Islam. They do not understand the mind of the Muslim, they have never studied the Qur'an and they do not understand what Muslims think of women. I believe we need to see more Muslim orientated training centres globally.

Flying by the seat of your pants is exciting but causes great insecurity. How are you to know that you are doing the right thing? By taking time to study and sit under godly men who have academic and spiritual insights you will have a confirmation of ministry.

5) Placement. Correct recruitment, screening, training and placing people in the right place is crucial to long term success. People might be quite stable in their own country but suddenly, when they go outside their own culture and lack their accustomed support mechanisms, they can fall apart. You can suffer a nervous breakdown and potentially severe culture shock. I know of one family who went to Pakistan. They were from England and the wife suffered severe culture shock. She reacted against everything that was Pakistani. She would even allow her little female children walk naked in front of Afghan men. She said: "These people have got to learn how to live in the real world". She revolted against the Pakistanis. It has taken many, many years for her to find a balance. So screening and placing people is a very important part of church planting. The right people being kept in the right way. How we keep people on the field is a vital issue. Placement requires finding the right people and having the full ability to pastor them on the field. Having sufficient back-up is essential.

6) Find someone who can think strategically; not all have a mind to do that. One dear friend was very frustrated by not being able to reach a tribe in Iran that he was called to. By talking it over with another strategic thinker a creative alternative was found to break the log jam.

7) Begin to learn the language. Language learning is the key to understanding the culture. If you know the language, you quickly get involved with the people. There are still missionaries on the field who have never learned the language. Learning the language leads to deeper involvement; you begin to integrate and to be like the people. I have met people who can do it in 3 months and I have met people who have never done it. Let me say that it is not only important just to learn the language but to learn the language in the way that the people speak it. Now this is very hard. Why? Because you have to become like a child, dropping any pride, which can be a humbling experience.

When I went to Iran, I learnt some Iranian words, drove out on a distribution team and started distributing literature. I used the phrases I had learnt. An Iranian said: "Oh, you speak beautiful Persian! How many years have you lived here!" I said: "I have been here only 2 months." Then I drove another 100 kilometres and did the same thing and another Iranian said: "Oh, you speak such beautiful Persian!" I thought: "Maybe I do!" In their culture they never say anything negative. They always say: "Oh, how wonderfully you speak". They never say: "You spoke that word wrong; this is the right way to speak it", unlike the Arabs. So some people may listen to the people and think: "Yes, I do speak good Persian or Turkish", but it is not true. If you speak you must also use the accent, the riddles and the jokes; that is hard, hard work.

So you must give yourself full-time to learning the language if you are going to stay there for a long spell. The measure that you get the language will be the length of time you spend in the country. If you do not get the language, you will get discouraged. You will give up and go home.

8) The place of aid and assistance. You must earn the right to speak. This, I believe, is what the Evangelical church has missed. Evangelical agencies have done the work, but churches have often failed to help their own local communities of poor and deprived. Those that have served their community have been blessed by it. We must get involved in aid, teaching, any other appropriate kind of assistance. How can we help people to live a better life? The Muslim will say to you: "Why are you here?" "My church sent me", you say: "I have come to tell you about Jesus." "How much money

do you get?" he asks; "My church sends me money to support me". So he says: "I will tell you about Muhammad for nothing. You tell me about Jesus because your church is paying you." So when you go to these countries they have to see that you have a reason for being there. You can be a student for only 4 or 5 years. What have you got to offer the people? How can you help them live a better life? I think we must return to balancing spiritual needs with people's practical needs. In the 19th and 20th century missions met the needs of the people by building schools, hospitals and places of health promotion. Today most governments cover these issues and the need is to find and create wealth for these nations both to feed their own people, to put them to work and to stave off poverty. Either by teaching marketable skills, developing export markets, or other such wealth creation schemes, we shall be of greater help to these new nations and their people. Even if none of them ever becomes a Christian, it is worth the effort, so that they might live a better life and a fuller one on this earth.

9) Disciple a few and build leadership. Today there is great emphasis on church planting and traditionally the church is founded upon the western missionary who is in place. If the western missionary gets thrown out of the country, the whole church collapses. What we have to see is the church being built around local leadership; the outsider who comes in must be making disciples. He must show faith in the local people and the Holy Spirit's ability to develop a situation. Too many times there are tribal problems between the people and our discipling must help them see that in Christ there is no tribalism. It will take a long, long process of intertribal healing and forgiveness for the church to grow.

The church and missions often go through phases and just now the subject on everybody's mind is church planting. Unfortunately the writers of most of the articles written and those speaking and advocating such a policy have never actually planted a church themselves. There is a severe credibility gap. Ask around; even mission leaders advocating church planting have never done it, not even in a western culture; some have never even witnessed to a Muslim, yet are challenging others to do it. My first piece of advice is NOT to try to do it. It is a most tough spiritual exercise and, unless there is a clear mandate from God and a gifting for the task, you will be crushed. In most countries there are churches that are engaged in establishing satellite churches, starting from cell groups, allowing them to grow into independent churches. Kensington Temple and Ichthus are two such movements in London itself. A period of internship and training within these structures would develop skills and produce insights that could be invaluable. Our own vision is to establish an International church in south London that can be a multi-purpose fellowship to serve that end - a centre of training, church life, and experience for those wishing to go overseas or stay in England in a cross-cultural environment. Whatever the method, we must realise that God blesses people and not programmes. He is looking for people willing to follow Paul and the apostles in their desire to make Christ known, to get to know the area and meet the needs of the people in practical ways of love and compassion, thus manifesting God's care and concern for them, and then also to find creative ways to present the truth that is found in Jesus Christ.

CHAPTER 11
Here's a Thought

Western missions are facing a mountain of difficulties that will cause us all to think, plan and pray more wisely regarding the evangelisation of the world in our time. The goal of world evangelisation in our generation may still be attainable, but not without radical readjustment of our thinking and commitments. One new aspect is that, excitingly, missionaries are now coming from all parts of the globe. Gone are the days when evangelism was in the hands of western churches alone.

Added to this, rising unemployment, recession, high bank rates and inflation have hit most of the major western sending nations over the past decade or more, but at the same time there is also an increased availability of workers because of unemployment, but this has had to be matched with a stricter screening, as more people are now coming from a dysfunctional family background. These new workers, however, often fall apart under the pressure of language learning, cross-cultural stress and loneliness on the field. After working in the Muslim world for thirty years I have come to the conclusion that God is never frustrated by these events. Often. He has been quietly working in the wings preparing the next phase of the work. Let us address the need to reach out in love, understanding and clear communication to the thousand million Muslims around this shrinking globe in a creative and alternate way.

As we have seen, the majority of Muslims fall into one of five cultural linguistic blocs. There are at least five Christian blocs that come from the same cultural linguistic backgrounds. People from these blocs can potentially identify more readily, live more cheaply and communicate more effectively than can western missionaries. The high cost of sending westerners is 'pricing out of the market' the massive use of Anglos. They will often last only ten years or less to return home for their children's education. They find it difficult to learn languages and to pastor them is a costly affair. The much vaunted 'Third force' in missions still sits waiting for the resources to enable them to take their full and rightful place in evangelising the world. Many of them are *near relatives* to the Muslim blocs identified above.

These new *near relatives* of the Muslims have neither the baggage of past imperialistic empires to contend with nor the present creeping imperialism and paternalism of America. They often actually come from an oppressed people themselves and therefore have a compatibility with their Muslim friend. One warning, however: we must not be naive in thinking that this will automatically work. A spirit-filled, loving American, German or Swiss is going to accomplish far more than a carnal Near Relative, in spite of his ability with language and simple lifestyle. It is also my observation that often the near relative concept breaks down when there has been too close an involvement with Muslims. For example, the Arab church has a long history of disappointment with Muslims. They feel they know the Muslim better than we and cannot bring themselves emotionally to reach out to them. Maybe they need to be distanced from the local scene and move to another interim place where they can learn neither to stereotype nor generalise the Muslim neighbour. Thus Egyptian believers could be placed in Morocco rather than Egypt to begin their exposure.

Then we need to look at the process that God uses, so that we can live with the temporary setbacks. In his notes on leadership Bob Clinton (Professor of Leadership at Fuller Seminary) lists 8 stages in a process that God allows a man or woman to go through. This process is in order to equip him better for the enormous task of being effective in fulfilling a vision. Visions do not lightly land on a person's shoulders. People have to grow and mature into the size that the vision demands. Jesus had His own men deny him, act treacherously, run away and fail Him utterly. You will also go through all the stages of life that Jesus went through if you are to take your place in the world struggle. He not only calls you to follow in His footsteps, but the one wanting to be conformed into His likeness He takes through the same process as He endured. This eventually leads to dying to self and trusting Him to raise you back again - a fearful experience.

Here are those eight stages;

1) The leader gets a vision of what God wants him to do. In this case it is to bring the message of the cross to Muslims and see fellowships develop. (Ask God to give you a vision of what He wants you to do.)

2) As he shares this vision, others feel that they also want to be involved and follow him. A team is built up and these new people learn from him. He becomes a model.

3) The leader and followers move along the suggested path. These are pioneering days and it is thrilling to see God meet all the needs. The work is often achieved in spite of lack of funds and resources. There is the thrill of seeing God provide in a miraculous way.

4) The demonic counter-attack comes and there are hard times, spiritual warfare ensues their ministry. This often takes place either just prior to or following a significant breakthrough. The team becomes poised to leap forward. The counter-attack or stress tests everyone. It is interesting that a number of missions went through major turmoil as the walls of communism fell and the doors opened for major growth. It was at that time that everyone felt unsure of which way to jump.

5) This results in a backlash from the followers, firstly against the strategy, but it quickly moves to the person and character of the leader. They had been part of the development of the strategy and therefore cannot deny what they have been part of developing. Funds are often lacking to take advantage of the new openings and frustration sets in.

6) The leader is driven to God to reconfirm God's call in the midst of this violent backlash. He is often thrown out of the ministry he started. This means that he must seek the face of God afresh as to what was his gifting and calling or whether he had deviated from it.

7) God reveals Himself further and makes it clear that the call is true. God's character as a faithful loving father is revealed and He then takes that man or woman to newer heights of understanding of Himself and the nature of the warfare.

8) Finally God vindicates Himself and the leader. The testing deepens the ministry and an expansion of the ministry takes place and goes to greater heights.

You can never be prepared for the bitterness and violence that is engendered by those who rebel against you, but you must only see it as God's way of widening your ministry. There comes a time when your vision must die, only to be reborn and confirmed by God in His resurrection power.

Whatever we do, there will be problems. These will be very different from what we are used to. They could be in the area of logistics, communications, value systems or family structures. To some English people the Celts are seen to be devious people. They never give a straight answer and are always seen to be beating about the bush. This is because they think differently. To answer directly is bad manners and offensive and thus miscommunication grows. Do not think that mobilising the Asian, African, Middle Eastern or Latin church is going to be easy but it will be worthwhile.

WIN believes that by adopting workers and churches within all of these Five Blocs western funds can release, for a fraction of the cost, better qualified men and women for this next thrust in Muslim world missions.

We must also ask: "Are westerners to have a role in this task of taking the gospel to Islam?" We must realise that the Muslim world must see the international, interracial nature of the church. However, western workers must come with the burden and vision to assist, train, encourage and serve the church and not to lead and control. This takes a very special kind of missionary who is willing to die to self so that others may run the race set before them. Can we approach Muslim missions on the basis of a global Church? Can we put resources at the disposal of these new missionaries for the fulfilment of their vision? Can we trust them to finish the task? It is a sad day if we cannot answer these questions with a resounding YES.

Hallelujah, our God reigns and He is doing a new thing in this final thrust in missions.

In summary, the proposition that we are in some way going to make a massive breakthrough in the Islamic world, as we have seen in the Communist world, is fraught with problems. This attitude comes more from triumphalism and ethno-cultural arrogance than from the spirit of God. In each age the church, and therefore missions, has been subtly infiltrated by worldly thinking. The age we live in now relies heavily upon management technique, manipulation of resources and, of course, a global marketing programme espoused by Madison Avenue and other philosophies. This is obvious to any one taking just a superficial glance at current mission hype about the Muslim world. We must return to a deeper awareness of the majesty of God, His working out of His purpose through the rise and fall of governments and leaders and the witness of the crucified life. It is this life that will bear witness to the work of the Holy Spirit; already at work in the Muslim world.

A return to intercessory prayer is essential. There was a time that The Fellowship of Faith for Muslims was considering closing down, such was the lack of interest in its ministry. We fought for a new commitment to prayer and God has kept it going. To close a prayer ministry for Muslims at a time when Muslims are more open today than ever in the past was madness. Today they are fulfilling a vital role in the mission's family.

We must never forget that, however good and logical the approach or method used to reach Muslims, it is men that God blesses and not methods. There must be a return to biblical spirituality with all that that means. Loyalty, justice, honesty, shame and sorrow are all but forgotten sisters in the characteristics of the modern evangelical. Too many are seeking to be the biggest, the sharpest, the most smooth running organisation and have lost sight of the fact that none of these really impresses a Muslim. It was the Muslim wandering holy man that walked out of the sand-blasted Sahara desert who impressed the Africans of Northern Nigeria, not the possessions of the visiting white missionary with his porters and equipment making him self-sufficient.

Our technical expertise is giving us an edge. Video, mass communication, film and the Internet are all being put to good use to get the content of the message out to the nations, but we still need to see men and women whose eyes are afire with the word of God, who are unstoppable and cannot be deflected from the task, enter into this last great act of the drama of the history of the world, a history which, since the beginning of time, has been focused on the plan of God for the nations and the conquest of His Son over evil.

CHAPTER 12

The following is a short reader on the subject of contextualisation. Wherever possible the authors have been contacted for permission to reproduce their work. My apologies to others to whom no credit has been given since we did not know who they were. Their papers were cast out on the sea of life.

Contextualisation

The Naaman Paradigm and Models of Survival
in the Middle East

David Zeidan

...When my master enters the temple of Rimmon to bow down and he is leaning on my arm and I bow there also - when I bow down in the temple of Rimmon, may the Lord forgive your servant this. "Go in peace," Elisha said (2 Kings 5:17-19).

The growing power of fundamentalist Islam in all Islamic states is a fact of life for Muslim believers in Jesus. Believers face growing pressures, harassment, persecution, imprisonment, even death sentences and execution. We have had such extreme cases in Pakistan and Iran and the tendency is spreading elsewhere.

We need a fresh look at the way the local community of Muslim believers ought to develop. Explicitly or implicitly we have often imparted a westernised model of Church structure and lifestyle to the local believers.

The danger is that if and when the full fury of Islamic fundamentalism coupled with state force is turned upon the fledgeling community it might completely disappear, many fleeing to the west for safety, others being martyred, as happened to the ancient churches in North Africa and Central Asia. I am talking here of Muslim believers, not believers from the nominal Christian churches, who, although under pressure, yet have legal status as people of the book. It is the Muslim converts who have no rights and are to be killed unless they return to Islam.

In order to ensure survival and even growth of the Muslim Followers of Jesus communities under persecution we must offer them a choice of various possible models. The visible part of the movement should be like the visible part of an iceberg - only one tenth in view above water, nine tenths invisible under the surface but obviously very much there!

The area of study that might yield valuable insights applicable to our day is that of Muslim sects who succeeded in propagating themselves and surviving under extreme forms of persecution. I suggest we study the extremist Shi'a (Alevis and similar groups) and the Isma'ili models, asking ourselves how these unpopular, unorthodox, state-persecuted groups succeeded in surviving and in propagating themselves. Another model would be that of a Sufi Tariqa. Tariqas are extremely widespread across the Muslim world and exhibit great variety in beliefs and forms, yet are accepted as within the Muslim fold.

Each area of study yields a model which can be applied and contextualised in our various fields today. Ideally, we ought to supply converts with several models adapted to the need of each specific country at a specific time and able to change to other models as needed.

Some General Guidelines:

Muslim believers desperately need a sense of identity. They need to be reassured that they are not traitors, heretics, western spies, etc. They must be able to have the firm conviction that they still belong to their people, culture, traditions, society - all that is good in their values that does not directly contradict the scriptures.

Muslim believers can claim that they are true Muslims for the following reasons:

a) Islam is not just a religion, but a civilisation. As such, all people living in its catchment area are Muslim in their culture, even if secular in their outlook or Christian in their religion.

b) Islam means submission to God. No one deserves this title more than Muslim believers who have submitted to God's revelation in His word and to His one way of salvation through Jesus by turning from any hope of gaining merit through their own efforts to hope for God's grace and mercy through the one atonement and mediator, Isa the Messiah.

c) All heretical Muslim groups claim they are the real Muslims, no matter what the orthodox establishment says about them. This is not deception - it is a firm conviction that they are the only faithful Muslims left in a world of apostasy. They are the chosen people, the remnant. Again, no one has a better claim to that than our Muslim brethren.

d) We do not expect the religious (or secular) authorities to accept this claim, but it is important for the believers to be able to make this claim for themselves with a clear conscience and great conviction and it will have an impact on their relatives, friends and contacts.

e) Contextualisation is possible, because many forms of Muslim worship and devotion are not contradictory to the Bible. Indeed, many are nearer the biblical models than those of western Christianity! We need to encourage believers to use Muslim terms and forms that can carry biblical meaning.

A Shahada for believers could say: "There is no God but God and Isa is His Messiah!" A truth no Muslim can deny! A famous Muslim scholar of the middle ages, al-Ghazali, stated that no Muslim could find fault with a Shahada that says: "There is no God but Allah, and Isa is his apostle", because it was a Qur'anic truth. Of course, he went on to say that Christians had turned Isa, the Messiah and apostle, into God, thus becoming polytheists. The fact remains that the statement is true and cannot be opposed by Islam.

The real problems are the person and status of Muhammad and the authority of the Qur'an. Here there can be no compromise, but they must be dealt with sensitively - these are not issues we need to emphasise or push - the enemy will do that to the best of his ability!

We are not talking about syncretism, but of Islamic forms which can be used and which Muslims recognise as their own. This may not save believers from persecution, but it may give them the inner confidence that they are part of their society, influence unbelievers to join them, and bring in an element of doubt and hesitancy in the

authorities' attitudes that could mean the difference between survival and annihilation.

All Shi'a groups have used the doctrine of Taqiya to survive in
a hostile environment. Western scholars disparagingly call it "dissimulation", giving the idea of deception. It may have been used in
that way, but in essence it means going underground in times of
danger. Concealing your faith from worldly authorities lest persecution wipe it out totally, keeping your faith hidden in public whilst
you practise it privately, not antagonising the hostile dominant
majority unnecessarily, conforming as much as possible to its ways
without renouncing your own convictions (Note: these are all things
that the early church, namely the first 3 centuries, practised). Multitudes of heretics were killed over the centuries; however, many
survived. This is what we need - a strategy for survival until the
storm is over!

The Alevis of Eastern Anatolia

Whilst official Turkish publications give the impression that 99% of
Turks are Sunnis, it is well known that at least 12 million Turkish
citizens belong to the Alevi minority. Because they belonged to the
same Islamic faith as the Shi'a Safavids of Iran, the enemies of the
Ottoman Empire, they came to be identified as heretics and apos-
tates by the Sunni Ottomans. They lived in an area that was the
battleground between the two rival empires, the one Sunni, the
other Shi'a, and it was their misfortune that the Ottoman Empire
proved stronger and prevailed over their territories, thus leaving
them as a despised minority, dangerous because allied religion-wise
to the enemy, in a dominant Sunni society. Many were massacred
in the 16th century. But even in 1978 in the southern Turkish city
of Kahramamaras a Sunni mob went on the rampage and slaugh-
tered scores of Alevis. The old hostility is always just beneath the
surface, and Alevis see themselves as a remnant persecuted for their
adherence to the true faith.

A remarkable fact is that most believers in Turkey come from
an Alevi rather than a Sunni background, indicating that the gulf
between their beliefs and Christianity is easier to bridge.

Ethnically they were identical with other Ottoman subjects -
mainly Turkoman and Kurdish - but the cleavage between them and

the Sunnis has persisted over the centuries and is still there for the perceptive eye to see in the modern Turkey of today. Theologically they are related to other extreme Shi'a groups in Turkey, Iraq, Iran and the Caucasus like the Yezidis, Ahl-i-Haq, Shabak, Kizilbash and others. Followers of the Bektashi order are usually thought of as Alevis too.

A main characteristic of Alevi belief is the elevation of Ali above Muhammad. For some, Ali is God, or part of a Trinitarian concept of God: God, Muhammad, Ali. In some versions Muhammad is replaced with Jesus; at other times Ali is said to be identical with Jesus. The concept is ambiguous and vague. Another aspect of Alevism is the rejection of the importance of external Muslim rites, stress being laid on the spiritual truths and devotion to God and right living (conduct). There may be a Christian background to some of these ideas.

In Alevi villages there is no mosque and minaret, no call to prayer. Some have mosques because forced to build them by Sunni authorities at some stage in the past, but then they are not well attended, if at all. Alevis do not keep the five pillars (unless forced to do so externally), consider the pilgrimage to Mecca an "external pretence" - the real pilgrimage is internal, in a person's heart.

Alevis meet privately in homes for their rituals, with their religious leaders, the Dedes, presiding. They celebrate a communion meal with wine, resembling the Christian communion. Travelling Dedes teach the faithful the basics of their faith.

Shared rites and traditions (rather than scholarship) determine Alevi identity and community. Alevism has certainly succeeded in self-renewal and survival. Their particularistic interpretations of Islam have not waned in modern times but maintain their vitality compared to the Sunni traditions.

What can we learn from the Alevis?

Underground church - Taqiyya - secretive about your faith, outward cultural conformity to the majority, inward clinging to own faith. Strong sense of community, marriage used as a strategy to strengthen the group - daughters are not given in marriage to unbelievers. Single fellows are provided with partners from within the community. Underground groups meeting in privacy of own home. Lay elders taking care of spiritual needs. Ability to transmit the faith orally to the next generation. We are the true Muslims, walking in God's way. Externals unimportant - faith and internal heart devotion central. Persecution to be expected by true believers, as God uses it to purify and strengthen them.

Isma'ili Small Cell Structure

In the early stages of Isma'ili development, when it was in extreme danger from the Sunni authorities, Isma'ilism developed an underground cell-like structure and a subtle and extensive missionary activity which helped them both survive and also propagate their particular faith all over the Muslim world. At one stage (9th-11th centuries) Isma'ilism almost managed to take over the leadership of Islam when the Fatimid Caliphate was established in Egypt. Early Isma'ilism functioned essentially as a secret society with an initiation ritual for admission. They are also said to have started the first Muslim trade guilds as a cloak for their activities.

Their main emphasis was on the distinction between the literal and the esoteric interpretation of the Qur'an. They follow the esoteric interpretation and view the literal interpretations and external commandments of Islam as irrelevant. Isma'ilism also had socio-egalitarian tendencies which appealed to the oppressed classes.

Isma'ili strength lay in its disciplined, hierarchical, secret organisation. It always seemed to have a cadre of indoctrinated and zealous members, eager to disseminate its doctrines.

The organisation was kept secret. Isma'ilis often held high positions in Sunni society, whilst keeping their membership secret. Like so many "moles" they burrowed under the whole Sunni system and often brought it near collapse when deeming the time ripe for a rebellion. Later, the Assassin branch of the Isma'ilis used assassination of its enemies as a political tool. The Druze are an offshoot of Isma'ilism.

What can we learn from the Isma'ilis?

Secrecy. Small secret cells may be the best hope of survival under extreme persecution. Ordinary members of a cell do not know the other cells - only the leaders know more, each according to his hierarchical level. Contacts are taught carefully under a promise of secrecy. Total secrecy rather than mere outward conformity is the rule. Communication is oral, nothing written is left behind. Converts continue holding high positions in society or penetrate into high positions without making their beliefs known, but wielding influence secretly on behalf of their brethren and faith. A wide network of missionaries is employed separate from the cell-structure of the movement. Every stratagem is employed to make the detection and infiltration of the movement difficult to the authorities. Plans are prepared for the day when the movement can openly take over society!

The Sufi Tariqa Model

Sufism is the mysticism of Islam. Ideally, it is an interior pilgrimage, leading away from the corruption of everyday life to the priority of union with God in a spiritual experience. Whilst the experience is individual, it is practised in a community of like-minded believers, thus amplifying the effectiveness of its faith and rituals. God's grace is manifested through the efficacy of a holy mediator, whose merit can be put to your account before God.

Sufism arose as a spiritual reaction to the legalism and worldliness of the religious establishment in the early days of Islam. It focused on men's quest for a personal and intuitive experience of God and used the techniques of asceticism, repetition of God's name and attributes, meditation and trance. Gradually it spread all over the Muslim world in the form of organised brotherhoods (Tariqas) and also had an important role in spreading Islam into new areas such as Central Asia, sub-Saharan Africa and South-East Asia.

Sufism is an infinitely complex matrix of multiple orders (Tariqas) that often exhibit similar structural frameworks whilst covering an immense variety of beliefs and practices, manifested in the wide spectrum stretching from sophisticated classical Sufism of the great masters to the obsession with baraka of the shrine and cult of saint Sufism popular amongst the poor masses.

The main characteristics that interest us are:

1. The external framework: Sufis meet in their own Zawiya for worship rather than in the mosque. Each Zawiya (local church) is headed by a Sheikh (elder, pastor) and several Muqaddams (servers, deacons). A Tariqa may have Zawiya branches in a small or larger region; some are international with branches in all Muslim lands, others are very small. It is this flexibility that is attractive!

2. The main Sufi ritual is the Dhikr (Remembrance), the goal of which is the remembrance of God according to His command. This is a close parallel to the regular communion service in obedience to: "This do in remembrance of me". Whilst the Sufi ritual of endless repetitions of God's name and attributes combined with ritual dance might appeal more to the Charismatics amongst us, it can certainly be modified to any balance of sobriety/ecstasy suitable to the individual group. The leaders keep strict control on members so that they do not stray from the balance accepted by their specific Tariqa. Some Tariqas have loud and vocal Dhikrs, other specify silent, internal meditation - so the field is wide!

3. Another Sufi ritual is the Sama' - a "concert" of poetry recitation, music and dance. This again can be adapted to music-loving evangelical needs!

In countries where Sufism is widely accepted, I propose we start a Sufi brotherhood within Muslim culture where people are known as followers of Isa, with Sheikhs (elders), Muqaddams (deacons), etc. Strong community spirit and meaningful rites help develop identity.

Dhikr will become the communion service and prayer meeting. Sama' will become the regular worship and Bible Study service.

4. Sufi Tariqas function also as mutual-aid societies. The poor get material help, the sick are prayed for, marriages are arranged, etc. Social interaction is strong in everyday life apart from the official gatherings.

The Problem of Alienation - Nibbling at the Fringes or Going for the Centre?

By David Zeidan

In examining our goals, strategies and results in evangelism, I'm struck by the fact that in most places where we work we're but nibbling at the fringes of the peoples we're trying to reach. I think it's time for us to re-examine some of our basic assumptions.

A basic hypothesis we've always held is that the local Church in every country can do the job if we just stimulate and train them to reach out to their own people. Underlying this hypothesis is the assumption that the local believers are much nearer culturally and missiologically to the indigenous target group than foreigners could be.

Through my personal experience in the Middle East and observation of other countries I have come to question this idea. I cannot offer simple solutions, but I think we must be realistic enough to recognise the problems and flexible enough to change our strategies and tactics accordingly.

Cultural gaps between various indigenous groups within a country can be quite large. This is especially true in Muslim countries of the gap between ancient Christian churches and the dominant majority. Between these two groups are centuries of prejudice that is extremely difficult to remove. The same is also true between the dominant majority and various other non-Christian minorities in the same country.

The following illustration is one way to show how these gaps (degrees of alienation) might be established between groups in a typical target field in the Middle East:

This country has ancient traditional Christian churches which are alienated by one degree from the majority group by centuries of oppression and deep-seated prejudices. The dominant majority group despises these Christians as eaters of pork and drinkers of wine, as immoral (especially in their treatment of women), as agents of the imperialistic West, as those who were led astray and did not accept the final truth of Islam. These Christians are protected as "people of the Book", but are oppressed and viewed as second-rate citizens, not "real" Arabs (or "real" Turks, Iranians, etc, depending on where you're working).

The Protestant churches, started by western missionaries in the 19th and 20th centuries, are a breakaway minority from the traditional churches and so are alienated by a second degree from the majority group.

The Evangelical churches are again a minority within the Protestant group, thus living in the third degree of alienation from the majority group. (Note: although the author does not name the Arab country he is talking about, he would be describing the exact situation in Egypt, Jordan, Syria and Lebanon.)

In an effort to strengthen the local church, some members of the evangelical church are recruited to work with an international mission agency which encourages them to adopt western lifestyles, thought patterns and social mannerisms, and then sends them abroad to rich western countries for training, deputation and fund-raising purposes. Unfortunately, when these people return home they become a minority within the already small evangelical church scene - envied and often ostracised by the real power centres in evangelical circles because of their easy access to foreign resources. They are seen as opportunist, seeking personal wealth and status. In this model they would belong to a sub-group that is four stages removed from the core community they are trying to reach with the Gospel.

In a real Middle Eastern state, Israel, the dominant Jewish majority also has complex sub-groupings of its own. There are gaps between the secularised majority and the large and powerful religious minority, between western and oriental Jews, and between political left and right. As there is no historical ancient church amongst the Jewish population, the Jewish believers (Messianic Jews) are either totally within their people sub-grouping, or at most only once removed from them culturally. They are ideal, in this model, for reaching other Israelis from similar backgrounds. Sad to say, there are western missionary-imposed divisions of theology and denomination at work in Israel, as well as the allure of easy money from churches and groups in the West. Yet the number of Israeli Jewish believers is growing exponentially.

On the Arabic side in Israel the Sunni Muslim group is the dominant group, with the main minority being the traditional Christian communities. Other minority groups are the Druze (a heretical offshoot of Islam) and the nomadic Bedouin. The overwhelming majority of Arabic believers come from the traditional (nominal) churches and from second or third generation Protestants and Evangelicals. They have so far been significantly unsuccessful in reaching out to their Muslim neighbours. Most of the handful of saved Muslims were won through western missionaries.

There are similar set-ups in most neighbouring countries like Syria, Lebanon, Jordan and Egypt. Whilst some of the Christians are gaining a vision for Muslim evangelism, their acceptability by the dominant Muslims is limited.

There is no simple and easy answer to this problem of alienation and how best to reach target people groups directly. I think we in OM need to ask ourselves some questions and think those issues through as we look at our mission strategies and at globalisation in the coming years.

Whilst I firmly believe in mass evangelism through literature distribution and other means, which prepares the ground and sows the seed in unreached populations, I also feel we need specialised long-term teams who will go for the centre, the dominant group, as well as other teams aiming directly at various minority groups within the centre. It is not a question of either/or, but both this and that. Our traditional ways reach out to the westernised groups in a given field - very often a minority of secularised people in the cities, but we also need to develop teams trained in methods of cultural adaptation and contextualisation to reach the centre of the people we're targeting.

If we can win some dominant group people and train them to evangelise within the cultural setting of their own people - not extracting them, but encouraging them to remain culturally a part of their group - their chances of doing the job, given the small or non-existent gap between them and their target, are much greater than the outreach of the alienated, western-trained evangelical.

Why Contextualisation in the Arab Middle East?   D. H.

Not that I am an "expert" or even one with "years of experience", but I feel I have some valid thoughts about the issue of
contextualisation as it pertains to reaching Arab Muslims with the
Gospel. My educational background includes a B.A. degree in
Cultural Anthropology, and Islamics and Contextualisation studies
at Fuller Seminary's School of World Mission. As for ministry
experience with Muslims, I started working with Arab Muslims in
1989 with Operation Mobilisation in London and continue to do so
currently in Jordan. Our strategy in London was, by and large, to
work "alongside" an existing Arab Christian Fellowship in reaching
the Arab Muslim population. This also happens to be my
organisation's overall strategy and approach to working with Muslims all over the world.

Tragically, my experience in London was the beginning of a
shocking discovery. I saw time and time again the way that Muslims
were treated when we brought them to church - namely like second
class citizens. I saw the overall unconcern amongst these "evangelical" Arab Christians in seeing the Muslims of London reached with
the Gospel. One of our tasks was to seek to "mobilise" the church
to do outreach. I can honestly say we saw more "fruit" in our
evangelism than we did in our "mobilisation" ministry. I began to
think that there must be another way. At this point, I must confess
that I have spent countless hours criticising Arab Christians and
their "lack of vision" to reach Muslims and God has really led me
to repent. Throwing "mud" accomplishes nothing. The purpose of
this short paper is not to "destroy" or "criticise" Arab Christians.
May God bless them, multiply their numbers and use them to win
"nominal" Christians to Christ. May He also raise them up to be a
"light" to their Arab Muslim brothers and sisters. What God has
encouraged me to do is to go about the task He has called me to
do - plant churches amongst Arab Muslims. The purpose of this
short paper is also not to discuss "contextualised" methodology, but
to present a basic apologetic for the approach.

The first question I want to look at is: how should we go about
accomplishing the task of planting churches? Traditionally my mission and most missions have sought to work alongside the "existing" church to reach Muslims. For example, I know of one worker

in Egypt who has been in the Arab world for about 25 years with the vision to "mobilise" Egyptian believers to reach Muslims - all along assuming that "they will be much more effective than we ever shall, because they know the language and they know the culture". It sounds like a solid approach, but of his own confession, after all these years he is only beginning to see some of the Egyptian believers really getting a vision to reach out to their Muslim brothers. I want to comment on three things in reference to this worker and his strategy.

Firstly, I personally have not been called primarily to "mobilise Arab Christians" to reach Muslims, but to reach Muslims. I also am firmly convinced that the ones who will be MOST able, and MOST burdened to reach Muslims are Muslims who have come to follow Jesus (I use the term Muslim followers of Jesus rather than "Christian" or "convert"). These are the muslims whom we need to pour our lives into and seek to mobilise. I guess you could say I am called to mobilise, but to mobilise muslims who are followers of Jesus.

Secondly, the assumption that Arab Christians possess the language and the culture is not AS TRUE as it may initially seem. Anyone who knows Arabic should know that the Arab Christians and the Arab Muslims have quite a bit of different vocabulary, especially when it comes to religious terminology. Many words that are used commonly by Arab Christians in religious matters are not at all understood by Arab Muslims and vice versa. Therefore any Arab Christian seeking to do outreach to Muslims needs to learn a lot of new vocabulary to communicate with Muslims - something that only a few, in my experience, have been willing to do.

As for the question of culture, from an anthropological standpoint the Arab Christian community, both evangelical and nominal, is clearly a distinct cultural entity. They see themselves as distinct from the majority population; they have many different customs and, as I have mentioned, they have a diverging vocabulary in certain areas. Just as one would classify the Hispanic community in Southern California as a distinct cultural entity from the typical white upper-middle class, so too we must see that not all Arabs are of the same culture.

The Muslim follower of Christ, however, has none of the disadvantages of the Arab Christian - he has exactly the same vocabulary, the same cultural background and furthermore, he doesn't have to overcome the distrust and spite that many Arab Christians unfortunately harbour for the Arab Muslim community, the understandable result of 1400 years of living under the heel of Islamic domination. At a human level, I can fully understand their feelings and distrust of the Muslim majority; however, from a biblical standpoint, we can't condone what amounts to a sinful attitude that demands repentance.

Thirdly, I need to comment on the issue of "investment". We, as workers in the Arab world, have only so many years to "invest" in the work of God. How are we going to invest? Is it a wise investment to spend 25 years to mobilise a handful of Arab Christians, or should we shift our focus to winning "a handful" of Muslims to Christ who will in turn be mobilisable to reach their own families, tribes, villages, cities and countries? It is in fact true that those "with the language and culture" will be more effective than the missionary, so let us seek to reach out to and mobilise those who really do have both the language and the culture - namely, Arab Muslims.

I believe we have been called to bear fruit and therefore should expect that there will be fruit as we serve the Lord in the Middle East. I have already seen that Muslim followers of Jesus are more effective in reaching their own, from both my ministry in London and here in Jordan. I believe we need seriously to consider that this is where we need to focus our efforts - winning and discipling Muslims to win and disciple other Muslims. Sure, there will be some Arab Christians who will be joining us, PRAISE GOD FOR THEM. Let's pray that those who do so will make the cross-cultural journey to be sensitive to Muslims by learning their vocabulary, adopting their cultural forms and not requiring more of Muslims who want to follow Jesus than Jesus did.

What do I mean by this last statement: "requiring more of Muslims....than Jesus did"? As one veteran worker in the Middle East has said: "I believe the overall strategy (of a certain organisation of which he was a member) in the Middle East, is a violation of the GRACE OF GOD". By that he meant that by telling a Muslim that he has to change cultures and become an "Arab Christian" in order to be a bona fide follower of Jesus, one is asking a Muslim do more than the Gospel requires. Most of us did not have to change our cultures in order to follow Jesus. I am still an American, and a Californian, and I happen to follow Jesus as well.

I think of one Muslim follower of Jesus who was being integrated into the Christian community here in Jordan. This person was told by Christian leaders here that he needed to change his vocabulary because now he was a Christian and Christians use these words. Understand that we are not talking about someone who used abusive language to a non-believer who needed to "clean up" his mouth as a follower of Jesus. No, we are talking about a Muslim follower of Jesus who was using the vocabulary that he grew up with to express himself and was being told to change to Arab Christian vocabulary. In my assessment, the tragic thing about this situation is that this individual was actually being made less effective to reach out to his own family and culture.

One point needs to be made about Arab Christian strategy to reach Muslims. There are some fine Arab brothers and sisters who have a heart to reach Muslims. I have worked alongside some very committed and gifted Arab brothers. I must confess that in almost every case, they would work with Muslims only on "their terms". What do I mean? Namely, that they were not seeking to be as culturally sensitive as they could to the Muslims they were reaching out to. By and large, they would not use Islamic religious vocabulary. Tragically, I saw them seeking to get Muslims to change their culture and become Arab Christians. They use Bible Translations that were made by and for Arab Christians with their unique Arabic Christian terminology which is largely not understood by the Muslim majority. And finally, most of them felt that Muslims have to be incorporated somehow into the existing Arab Christian Church. Praise the Lord, that even with all these "extra" requirements and barriers ("extra" meaning more than "believe on the Lord Jesus Christ and you shall be saved") there are Muslims coming to Christ, God is blessing and all over the world there are Arab Muslims in Arabic Christian Churches. Sadly, I wonder how many more would have come to know the Saviour if these obstacles had been removed.

When we look at church history, especially very early, we see an interesting development, which, I believe, is very relevant to this issue. Without getting heavily into the exegesis of certain passages, you could say that the early church was fundamentally divided into the Hebraic Jewish believers, the Hellenistic Jewish believers and the Gentiles. The first group was of those in Jerusalem, people like James and Peter, who were very Jewish in their thinking and customs. Many viewed them as a sect of Judaism. Although followers of Jesus, they remained very "Jewish". If someone who wasn't a Jew wanted to follow Jesus, they for the most part would want that person first to become like a Jew in order to follow Jesus. For example, they were told not to eat things that the Mosaic law forbade, to be circumcised, etc., etc. Jews who lived outside Palestine made up the second grouping. They were Jews who were heavily influenced by Greek thought. They were really kind of halfway between the two groups. The apostle Paul would have been most comfortable in this category. Although he was a "Pharisee of Pharisees" he would have been much more Greek in his thinking than a Hebraic Jew like James. The third group were those who were not Jews at all, or pagans, to use a less pleasant term. After my discussing this issue with a friend with considerable knowledge of the Jewishness of the early church, he explained that the churches of the first group, the Hebraic Jewish Christians, existed into the 4th century and eventually died out as a distinct entity. Eventually Christianity became by and large "Gentile/Pagan" in its membership and it was this "Gentile/Pagan" church that really evangelised the world. While the first group of believers were more inwardly focused toward Jerusalem and its environs, Paul and others were evangelising the regions beyond, becoming "all things to all men".

Why this short interpretative chronicle of early church history? Because we need to learn from it. The existing Arab Christian Church is more inwardly focused - and their primary target of outreach is nominal Christians. They are also very concerned with "matters of the law", cultural things they see as vital to be a "bona fide" follower of Christ. In order to join them, like the Hebraic Jewish believers of the initial centuries, you must become "like them". Interestingly enough, it was not this church that God used to evangelise the world in the earliest days of Christianity. Rather

He used a man, Paul, who, because he came from a middle position, was able to "set aside" his Jewishness in order to preach the Gospel of Grace. The fact is, a very Jewish Church would have never taken over the Roman Empire. Rather, what was needed was a church that could come into a culture and "contextualise" its methods and forms. If you examine many of our "Christian traditions" from the Christmas tree to our style and order of worship in the church, to the names of the days of our week, the time of year we celebrate Christmas, to the clergy/laity distinction, etc., etc. - you will discover that they are "ALL" of pagan origin. Shocking? It just goes to show that God can use existing cultural forms, redeem them and use them for His purposes and His glory.

Paul wrote: "I make myself a slave to everyone, to win as many as possible. To the Jews I became like a Jew, to win the Jews. To those under the law I became like one under the law (though I myself am not under the law), so as to win those under the law. TO THOSE NOT HAVING THE LAW I BECAME LIKE ONE NOT HAVING THE LAW (though I am not free from God's law but am under Christ's law) so as to win those not having the law. To the weak I became weak, to win the weak. I HAVE BECOME ALL THINGS TO ALL MEN so that by ALL POSSIBLE MEANS I might save some" (1 Cor. 9:19-22 - NIV, emphasis mine).

In the first draft of this paper I was criticised for saying that "Paul became a Greek to win the Greeks". What I should have said to be absolutely precise is that, although himself a Jew, he "became like one not having the law" and that he had "become all things to all men". When Paul said he "became like one not having the law", he was saying that he became "like" a Greek. Quoting one commentator concerning 1 Corinthians 9:21, "those not having the law, (refers to) those who have not been raised under the OT Law (the Gentiles) ... Paul accommodated himself to Gentile culture when it did not violate his allegiance to Christ" (W. Harold Mare, NIV Study Bible, Zondervan Bible Publishers).

As for Islam and the Muslim World, I believe we need, as Paul did, to become "like one not having the law" or, putting it in another way, we need to become "like Muslims for the Muslims". If the Arab Muslim world is to be evangelised like the 1st, 2nd and 3rd century world, the church will need to be a lot less "Christian" and a whole lot more "Muslim". Many of the Islamic forms, for example, the way they pray (both kneeling and bowing), their strong emphasis on fasting for all believers, even praying in a specific direction are all MORE BIBLICAL than most of our present evangelical practices. (There have been Jews since O.T. times who face Jerusalem when they pray. We read in the O.T., "...Daniel....went home to his upstairs room where the windows opened TOWARD JERUSALEM. Three times a day he GOT DOWN ON HIS KNEES and prayed, giving thanks to his God, just as he had done before." Dan. 6:10 NIV, see also 2 Chronicles 6:38.) It is also interesting to note here that the first Muslims in Medina adopted the Jewish habit of facing Jerusalem and praying 3 times a day. (This is the Qibla, or direction of prayer, which I am practising and advocating for Muslim followers of Jesus.)

These and other forms that Muslims use are all more than "redeemable". Many seem to have the perspective that since something is Islamic it is satanic and we need to abandon it completely. The early Christians testify to the fact that many pagan forms were not only NOT considered "satanic" but actually incorporated into the body of Church life, and we use them to this day.

In conclusion, for those who think contextualisation is some "new Missiological" idea of the past few decades, I would challenge them to read again Acts of the Apostles and Paul's epistles. I would challenge us to think about whether we are actually violating the Grace of God by asking Muslims to do more than believe in order to be saved. Although Paul had his problems with the leadership in Jerusalem at times, and they had their problems with him to be sure, they, in a spirit of unity, were able to bless one another and accept each other and what they perceived to be "God's calling" on their lives. Tragically, there is little unity today between those who are in the church and work with the church and those who believe they need to work outside the church and to become "like Muslims to reach Muslims".

I would say at this point that I too am a realist. Just as James and Peter in Jerusalem never became "like one not under the law" God used them and blessed them but you cannot say they "turned the unevangelised world upside down" either. Some Arab Christians, may become like Paul and be willing to give up their culture, and traditions to reach their Muslim neighbours. However, let us not forget that it took a Damascus road experience and then many years in the "wilderness" to prepare him for that calling. From what I have seen, these individuals will be exceptions rather than the rule. I know that the Arab Christians will continue to reach out to Muslims in their own way, and as a result certain Muslims will be willing to change cultures and join them. In Jerusalem some non-Jews undoubtedly became like Jews to follow the Messiah. Unfortunately those Hebraic Christians couldn't really accept those who weren't willing to do just that. The evidence suggests that Arab Christians, like those early Hebraic Christians, are for the most part unwilling to accept Muslims unless they become Arab Christians.

God used "contextualised" churches to reach the world in the beginning, and I believe this is how He is planning to reach the Arab Muslim world now. Will they ever call themselves "Christians"? Probably not. The early followers of Christ were first "called" Christians at Antioch but they didn't use that term to describe themselves until much later. As Mark Harlan has written, "the followers of Christ did not identify themselves as 'Christians' in the time of the New Testament, and consequently there is no biblical necessity for us to use this term to describe our identification with Christ" (Harlan, "Contextualized Identification"). Rather, it was a term used by non-believers to describe the followers of Jesus. (If anyone desires a thorough investigation of the early believers' identity, I would direct them to the paper by Mark Harlan of IMI, entitled "Contextualized Identification".) They called themselves "followers of the way" or "the way of God/the Lord".

Will they meet in places called "churches"? Probably not. Messianic Mosques, Messianic Majlises, or whatever. Who knows? They will have met the Messiah and will find their lives in Him and they will try to be relevant to their neighbours and friends in order to win them too. The Spirit of God is big enough to "guide (them) into all truth" (John 16:13), just as He has led us. Will there be problems? Heresy? Extremism? Probably; church history is a testimony to these things. One thing, however, is that the ONLY STUMBLING BLOCK must be Jesus Himself. Not another culture, or another identity or whatever. Jesus is a big enough obstacle. If a Muslim chooses not to follow the Messiah, let's make sure that it isn't because of extra things that have been added to the Gospel of Grace, but because of Jesus alone.

In conclusion, I realise that what I have written has offended some. The first draft of this paper was given to some friends to critique and to give their reactions and comments, and somehow it got into the hands of some other people before I was able to incorporate the criticism and suggestions that my fellow co-workers made. Several of my readers felt that the paper had an "underlying attitude" which wasn't right. I have tried my best to change that. I make no apologies that this paper is advocating a contextualised approach to reaching Muslims. As I have stated, I am convinced that this is the best way forward in the Arab Muslim world. I am also keenly aware that there are many who disagree with my convictions and the convictions of others who are moving into more contextualised means of Muslim outreach. I believe God has called different people to different ministries. Not everyone feels led to be involved in "church planting". Some feel God has called them to work with and through the existing church. My goal is not to try to discredit other people's ministries. Some of my close friends in my own organisation have said that I have made them feel "as though their ministry wasn't valid". I want to say that this has not been my intention. Strongly as I feel about contextualised church planting outside the existing church, I do believe God has led and is leading some to work alongside the existing church. I want to bless those of you who have that specific calling. I am not questioning that God is blessing and using the Arab Christian Church in Muslim outreach. I pray that we shall see much more happening in this area. I would ask the question, however, as to why the majority of workers seem to end up in that ministry. Would God not want many more to be involved in pioneer church-planting ministries? Rather than criticise one another's ministries, I hope and pray we can bless one another and agree to disagree.

For a discussion as to why I believe we can call ourselves "Muslims" without being deceptive, I would direct the reader to another paper I have written - "The Issue of Deception in Contextualized Identity"

Why are We Stuck in The Mud of Contextualisation?

An inquiry into a case of unapplied contextualisation — by M.H.

For over a decade our organisation has had a clear and biblically sound policy which affirms a commitment to contextualisation. I should love to think that we are on the 'cutting edge' of developing and applying contextual theory within the bounds of a solid biblical and theological framework, but, though we have an excellently worded policy, there is seemingly little awareness of its existence. Furthermore, when invited to present a paper on the subject of contextualisation for this conference, I was informed by someone in leadership that this topic was not a 'hot' one for many in our organisation. In fact some had objected to having it on the docket at all, viewing it as irrelevant. Nevertheless, I realise that many would agree with the aims of contextualisation and others would say that they are contextualising their ministry to some degree. Yet, if I may freely express my opinion, it is my judgement that we are not pursuing the matter very vigorously. To my knowledge, until now little attention and effort has been devoted to this cause.

In this paper I should like to discuss some of the possible reasons for this state of affairs. I would suggest the principal causes to be the following: (1) our insensitivity to the Divine imperatives for contextualisation and our ignorance of / ignoring of biblical teaching on the issue; (2) fear of compromising biblical truth and standards, which leads, ironically, to our propagating an opposing heresy; (3) fear of syncretism as well as unscriptural conceptions of what it is; (4) an excessively negative view of Islam that leads to extractionism; (5) our conservative roots (theological, social, political and personality) that hinder us from taking risks or exercising creativity; (6) wrong priorities and unwillingness to pay the price; (7) ethnocentric ignorance of the history of contextualisation in western Christianity and (8) a lack of leadership, pioneers and modelling. Let me elaborate on these causes:

1. Insensitivity to God's radical commitment to contextualised incarnational communication

Contextualisation is not some new missiological theory out of Pasadena, rather it is a commitment to faithfully following the divine model for communication. Numerous examples of it could be given

from both the Old and New Testaments, but the supreme example
is the incarnation. In it God accepted the constraints and risks of
limited communication and communicated Himself in Christ, without compromise, to humanity. All valid contextualisation is but a
reflection of this principle.[1] It is essential that we realise that God
is a receptor-orientated communicator who goes to extreme measures in order to communicate in ways that convey meaning to men.
One observer comments:

In Jesus, God's desire to be understood as relevant and important to contemporary human life led him to so contextualise himself
as a human being that He was not even recognised by most of the
people of his day. He looked too human . . . .[2]

Our God is committed to incarnational communication.

He speaks the language of the people He seeks to reach, even
disrespected languages like Galilean Aramaic and *koine* (common)
Greek. He even uses the cultural practices of pagan societies to
communicate His message to those living in them.[3]

The prophets often model this divine pattern of contextualisation.
Excellent illustrations of this are found in Hosea and Amos. In
order to reveal God's anguish over a spiritually adulterous people,
God ordered Hosea to marry an "adulterous woman". The marriage
produced three children to whom Hosea gave names which
symbolised the imminent judgement of the nation. Later He com-
manded him to "love a woman living in adultery", to show that God
still loved His people, despite their religious harlotry.

James L. Mays describes this "contextualisation," as follows:

[Hosea] had to "incarnate" in his own personal life the word of
Yahweh. That he could and did is evidence of his profound identification with his God, an identification which, if we can judge
from his sayings, allowed him even to feel and experience "the
emotions of Yahweh".[4]

---

[1]Arthur Glasser, Old Testament Contextualization: Revelation in Its Environment", The Word Among Us, Dean Gilliland ed. (Dallas: Word), p. 49.

[2]C. Kraft, Word, Contextualizing Communication, The Word Among Us, Dean
Gilliland ed. (Dallas: Word), p. 122.

[3]*Ibid.,* p. 126.

[4]Quoted by Arthur Glasser, Ibid., p. 42.

Why did God go to such an extreme in ordering Hosea to act so? Did He not realise that some believers (and even Bible scholars) would stumble over Hosea's conduct, while unbelievers would attack this revelation on the basis that a righteous prophet could not possibly leave such a scandalous example for the godly to follow? The answer seems to be that our God is committed to be relevant and powerful through incarnational communication.

Then we have the example of Amos who so creatively incarnated his messages through Israel's culture.

Amos knew the art of appropriating a variety of speech-forms as the vehicle of what he had to say. His speeches display a remarkable skill at using all the devices of oral literature available in Israel's culture. He sang a funeral dirge for Israel in anticipation of its doom (5:1-2) and formulated woe-sayings as a way of marking certain kinds of action as those which lead to death (5:18; 6:1; 5:7). He used several forms that belonged to the priest to mimic and attack the cult of the nation (4:4f; 5:4, 21-24). He was especially adept at the employment of forms of speech that appear in the riddles, comparisons and popular proverbs of folk wisdom.... He argued with the logic of proverbs (3:3-6) and used comparisons and riddles to make his point (2:9; 3:12; 5:2,7,19, 24; 6:12; 9:9).[5]

May I assert that if we are not aggressively pursuing contextualisation in our communication and ministry, then we are failing in our sonship by not reflecting the image of our Father? One missiologist goes so far as to say: "If God's message is not contextualised, then it ceases to be true to what God intended and becomes to some extent heretical."[6] I pray that each of us will re-evaluate his attitude and commitment to contextualisation in light of our God, the archetype of incarnational communication.

2. Fear of compromising biblical standards and truth

Many begin to feel uneasy when the subject of contextualisation is brought up, suspecting that it will eventually lead to compromise and/or deception. Certainly, we must follow the example of the apostolic band of Paul, who stated: "We have renounced secret and

---

[5]*Ibid*, p. 42.
[6]Kraft, p. 122.

shameful ways; we do not use deception, nor do we distort the word of God. On the contrary, by setting forth the truth plainly, we commend ourselves to every man's conscience in the sight of God" (2 Cor. 2.2). While some seem to associate contextualisation with deception and distortion, the goal of contextualisation is in fact to "set forth the truth plainly". It is not enough to avoid syncretism, but we must also communicate relevantly and clearly - and the only way we can achieve that is through contextualisation. To concern ourselves with one at the expense of the other is to be unfaithful to our biblical responsibility. Zeal in contextualisation and regard for moral integrity are not incompatible, for the same apostle who was supremely committed to integrity was also the most committed to contextualisation:

"To the Jews I became as a Jew, that I might win Jews; to those who are under the Law, as under the Law, though not being myself under the Law, that I might win those who are under the Law; to those who are without law, as without law, though not being without the law of God but under the law of Christ, that I might win those who are without law. To the weak I became weak, that I might win the weak; I have become all things to all men, that I may by all means save some.[7]

3. Fear of syncretism, which is often unscriptural in its conceptions and leads to the promoting of an opposite form of it.

Out of a concern to avoid syncretism we find those who argue against the use of forms which are contaminated by non-Christian or pagan usage. Many thus judge various Islamic forms to be unacceptable, because of unbiblical associations. This type of objection may seem logical, but we find that it does not seem to be of overriding concern to the Holy Spirit. For example, El was the basic name for God in the Ancient Near East and was the name of the supreme god of the Canaanite pantheon. Yet the Holy Spirit appropriated it and gave it new meaning and used it as one of the Divine names in the Old Testament revelation. (The use of the plural form Elohim with singular meaning was not unique to Israel either).[8] Furthermore, if inaccurate or pagan conceptions associated with

---

[7] 1 Cor. 9:20-22.
[8] Glasser, p. 36.

forms render them unusable, we should be astonished to find that the New Testament writers, along with the Jewish translators of the Septuagint, chose *theos* from the Greek pantheon to refer to YAHWEH, the God of the Bible. Let us examine the ideas the Greek world associated with the term *theos*.

The Greek religious concept of *theos* was polytheistic in the sense of 'an ordered totality of gods' which brought into prominence and found its finest expression in the person of Zeus. *Theos* was also used for Apollos, Athena, Eros, etc. and even the cosmos was called God, not to mention heroes and outstanding rulers. Although "eternal" they came into being like men from the same mother. *Theos* did not create the world out of nothing, but are merely the attainment of order and form. The influence of the gods was not universal, but limited. They were not righteous in the biblical sense. They had human form. The Greek religious conception of God could hardly be described as biblical. Neither could its philosophical concept be done so. In Greek philosophy god was not personal, though the divine forms were spiritualised and replaced by concepts like 'world reason' and 'being'. "There does not enter into the Greek mind any thought of a 'deity' whose innermost essence is love, love for man and not merely for individual elect."[9] The pagan concepts associated with *theos* and the high potential for miscommunication would have seemed to many of us to make its use as a form 'unredeemable', yet the NT writers chose to use it and transformed it, not having the shape and form of the pagan conception, but as pure spirit.[10]

A similar concern might be raised over John's use of *logos* (the word), in referring to Christ's deity and incarnation. J. D. Pentecost asserts that John's concept of the logos does not adopt either the Old Testament concept or that of the Jewish philosopher Philo. He quotes Shaped who states:

[9]Kittel's Theological Dictionary of the New Testament , s.v. "Theos".

[10]Glasser, p. 36. Some may presume that because of use in the Septuagint the term would have been well-defined by New Testament times, but this would have been true only of those Gentiles who had detailed knowledge of Judaism. When the apostles preached to the Gentiles in Acts, their hearers would have had in mind the common pagan notions in regard to theos, but then they would correct misconceptions about Him, as Paul did with the philosophers of Athens (Acts 17: 23-31).

His idea of the Logos was not that of Marcus Aurelius, the generative principle in nature, nor that of Philo, the Divine Reason and Expression, nor merely that of the Hebrew *memra*, the manifestation of God as the Angel of Jehovah or the Wisdom of God, but the religious idea of the Divine Word, creating, revealing, redeeming. John seized upon the terminology of current Greek thought and filled it with a new content ....He reproduces with new content various phases of the Platonic conception (emphasis mine). [11]

Thus the Apostle John appropriates a familiar term, but modifies it, giving it a new meaning.

Then we have the Holy Spirit inspiring the Apostle Paul to search for terms from the mystery religious cults to communicate gospel truth. One missiologist observes: "It could be somewhat disconcerting, even today, to admit that Paul went into the local religions to find ways to teach Christ, but this is surely part of the reason why God chose him as the apostle to the gentiles." Such words include: "minister" (leitourgon) in Rom 15:16 and "libation" (thysia) and "sacrifice" (leitourgia) in Phil 4:18.[12] Another example is Paul's choice of *katallasso* (reconcile) and *katallage* (reconciliation). These terms were familiar to the Greeks in regard to resolution of the tensions between people and the pagan gods, whereas the more acceptable way of communicating the mediating work of Christ to the Jewish mindset would have been *hilaskesthai* (to propitiate or make expiation for), as in Heb. 2:17, but Paul never uses it.[13] Though some of us may have felt uncomfortable adopting expressions that had always been so closely associated with pagan cultic practices, the Apostle to the Gentiles adopted, adapted and transformed them into dynamic vehicles of communication.[14] Paul searched for language and expressions that conveyed truth with the highest degree of local impact. By doing so he demonstrated that:

---

[11]J. D. Pentecost, Words and Works of Jesus Christ (Grand Rapids: Zondervan, 1981), p. 29.

[12]Dean Gilliland, "New Testament Contextualization: Continuity and Particularity in Paul's Theology", The Word Among Us, edited by same author (Dallas: Word), p. 56.

[13]*Ibid.*, pp. 55-56.

[14]*Ibid.*, p. 56.

The gospel will be a living faith only as it takes seriously the concrete values and dynamic issues raised by each culture. In general, the Jews balked at a reframing of the order and terminology. They would rather have an abhorrence of what might become syncretism, should the gentiles be given too much liberty. Yet if this liberating gospel had become imprisoned within Jewish belief and practice, the result would have been a Jewish brand of syncretism. This, in fact, almost happened. Paul had to fight Judaistic distortions through his correspondence on at least two occasions.[15]

If we substituted the word "Christians" for "Jews" and "Muslims" for "gentiles", the above quote would well describe the unwittingly accepted development of "Christian" syncretism so prevalent among our fields today. In our zeal to avoid syncretism and compromise we too often have promoted another type of syncretism, that is, expecting or requiring Muslims to reject their own forms and adopt "Christian" ones. Our attitude toward believers from Islam is very much like the first century Jewish believers' toward Gentile believers. Yet this was perhaps the fundamental issue at stake in ecclesiology and soteriology in the New Testament.

The point of Acts 15 is that those from a non-biblically based cultural-social-religious background have the right to hear, believe and follow Christ without sacrificing their heritage and without having to adopt that of those from a biblically rooted cultural-religious background. If we do not allow them this right, then we are "Judaising the gentiles" and promoting heresy and "Christian" syncretism. Heresy and syncretism are not just matters of what we teach and preach, but they can equally be propagated by what our practice of missiology communicates to other cultures. In Galatians, Paul records his public rebuke of Peter, not for preaching heresy, but for not practising the gospel of grace in his withdrawing from eating with uncircumcised Gentile believers under pressure from Hebrew believers. Such conduct was condemned by Paul as not being "straightforward about the truth of the gospel" (2:16) and tantamount to "nullifying the grace of God" (2:21). When we expect Muslims to come out of their Islamic culture and society and identify with "Christian" customs and community, we nullify the

---

[15]*Ibid.*, p. 58.

grace of God which accepts the Muslim believer on the basis of his allegiance to the Messiah alone and we compromise the truth of the gospel which saves "gentile" Muslims without requiring them to become "Christians". In our concern to avoid syncretism we too often have committed the opposite heresy: limiting or distorting the gospel by holding on to a form, even though the meaning is lost.

We should note here that even forms which we consider "sacred" may be contextualised and still preserve their meaning. This is evident from the New Testament authors' use of the Jewish Greek translation of the Hebrew Old Testament (the Septuagint). When quoting from the new form, they still referred to it, under inspiration of the Holy Spirit, as the "Word of God". This is the ultimate proof of the fact that new forms can be every bit as "holy" as the original ones. (Contrast this with the Islam's insistence upon the untranslatability of the Qur'an and upon the reciting of the prayers in Arabic by non-Arabs.)

In summary, we find frequent and astonishing use by the writers of inspired Scripture of local forms which have negative and unbiblical associations and high potential for miscommunication, distortion and even syncretism. Yet the Holy Spirit shows little reluctance to adopt those familiar and relevant local forms and then sanctify them for His use in significant communication by filling them with new content. His priority seems to be the relevance and familiarity of forms, which He then fills with new meaning and relies on teaching to clarify the different meaning and reduce the danger of syncretism.

Thus it has been stated: "The good news is something that Jesus died to give the world. Paul, therefore, cannot demand that people accept what is alien to them or what they do not understand."[16] Also: "The good news for people everywhere is that the Word became flesh and, speaking contextually, the Word must become flesh again and again to each locale and for every people".[17]

---

[16]*Ibid.*, p. 58.
[17]*Ibid.*, p. 52

4. An excessively negative attitude towards Islam

This attitude which is so prevalent among Christian workers is another factor working against contextualisation. Islam is viewed as an "evil empire", a satanic system of oppression, bondage and darkness; as a result, many feel that the gospel itself requires the rejection of everything associated with Islam, even if it involves extractionism, but the controversial question, as pointed out by John D. C. Anderson nearly two decades ago, is whether the concept of a "Christian Muslim" (or "Jesus Muslim") is valid.

Is it possible for a man to be a child of God, a worshipper of Christ, and yet still to fall under the broad national and cultural category of being a Muslim?...There are many experienced Christians who would regard it as blatant compromise or as a form of religious syncretism, but our need is to differentiate between the traditional concept of making a Muslim into a Christian, with all the transfer of his loyalties to an imported Christian sub-culture that this involves, and, in contrast, that of making him into a disciple of Jesus Christ, with a primary loyalty to Him as Saviour and Lord from amidst his nationalities. His headlong confrontation with conservative Muslim theology will come sooner or later, but may he have enough time to demonstrate to his family and friends that the servant of Christ is neither a blasphemer of Allah nor a traitor to the best interests of his country, but in the highest possible sense one who submits himself to the will of God (which is what Islam means)? Thus the emphasis we are trying to make is upon the Muslim and his culture being changed from within. It was just in such a way that our western culture has been changed from within, when once the transforming Gospel made its entree. This approach is not currently accepted by the western Church. It is contended here, however, that its implications need much closer study. In any case, what are we to say of the fact that our traditional approach to the Muslim has been so singularly unproductive? In the past a convert from Islam has been seen by his fellow countrymen only in a negative light as one who throws out Islam in toto. Whereas in fact there is much in Islam that appeals to the conscience of good men....The issue is really where the ultimate spiritual battle is to be fought. Is it to be inside Islam, or outside? In the one case a few expelled converts try, if they have the courage, to persuade their erstwhile Muslim friends to leave Islam and to join the Christians. In the other, a thousand earnest disciples, with varying depths of spiritual perception, are asking questions within Islam, which may ultimately shake it to its foundations.[18]

Unfortunately, even since Anderson wrote in the 70's, the majority of missions effort seems to have changed little, judging by the recent article in a missions journal: "Is extraction evangelism still the way to go?"[19] The author notes the dichotomous dealings of missions of the church in India between tribal works, where missionaries are expected as much as possible to develop churches as an integral part of tribal society, and high-caste Hindu and Muslim outreaches, where individuals are called to profess Christ and join the Christians, extracting them from home and society and destroying bridges for the gospel. Not surprisingly, tribal outreach is much more successful, whereas the worker states that there is no present effectiveness in winning Hindus and Muslims. While we must be concerned about avoiding compromise with Hindu and Muslim cultures, we need to take note of the elasticity of these cultures in tolerating renegade religious elements. He exhorts us that:

> The presence of anti-idolatry movements within Hinduism should make us pause. Why can an educated Hindu reject idol worship and stay in his home (usually not without problems), while those who under Christian influence reject idolatry are expelled? The same applies to caste, which many modern Hindus are defying to various extents.[20]

A double standard is likewise apparent if we note the widespread acceptability of the approach of "Jews for Jesus". Yet many supporters of the former are critics of a "Muslims for the Messiah" movement. The difference, they say, is because Judaism was a true religion or that it is based on divinely inspired Scriptures. Yet neither New Testament nor modern rabbinic Judaism could accurately be said to be a true religion, nor are they really based on the Word of God. Jesus constantly attacked Judaism as sophistry and a sham.

---

[18]John D. C. Anderson, "Our Approach to Islam: Christian or Cultic?", Muslim World Pulse, 6 (Feb. 1977), pp. 4-5.

[19]H. L. Richard, "Is extraction evangelism still the way to go?", Evangelical Missions Quarterly 30, No. 2 (April, 1994), p. 172.

[20] Ibid.

He said that it was based on the traditions of men which were given even greater authority than the Scripture. The teachings of modern Judaism likewise are based much more on non-scriptural sources than they are upon the Old Testament. We should remember that the Qur'an's oft-stated purpose is to confirm the message of the Bible and about 70% of its content is from it. If it be argued that Islam is not a divinely sanctioned religion, the same can be said of "Christianity". Where do we find the religion "Christianity" in the Bible? Nevertheless, the crux of the matter is not a comparison between Judaism and Islam, but rather the clear teaching of Acts 15! The crucial point agreed upon by the Jerusalem Council was that those from a community with a non-biblically based religious heritage (Gentile paganism) did not need to convert to the existing communal identity, i.e. (Messianic) Judaism. They could remain Gentiles who followed Christ! (And let us not overlook the fact that to be a Gentile was to be religious and Gentile religious affiliations were overwhelmingly pagan!) That being the case, how much more acceptable is it for Muslims, who are not pagan, but profess to be monotheistic believers in the Holy Scriptures, to retain their Islamic communal identity!

There are other reasons for our excessive hostility toward Islam and for our following extractionist methodology. Anderson's startling analysis suggests that the primary factor that causes us to respond to Islam as "western cultic Christians" is that we are rigid and proud. We feel our churches are nearest the N.T. pattern. We can't work well with those who hold to different viewpoints - e.g. on baptism, tongues, vestments or Calvinism. Our pride is evident in the negative attitude we have toward Islam, because it has so dogmatically taught doctrines contrary to our faith and has withstood Christianity so successfully - in spite of dedicated and godly Christian witnesses - this hurts and rankles with us and our pride is also evident in our difficulty in empathising with Muslims:

That ability to accept their persons, their feelings and their right to believe as they do - a gift we must have if we are to succeed in identifying with Muslims as fellow-sinners in need of a Saviour. We may not agree with them; we may think they are deceived and hold erroneous teaching, but we must "accept" them and "accept" Islam as the culture into which, by God's will they were born. Jesus "accepted" humanity and identified with it in His Incarnation. More than that, He, though pure and sinless, even identified with sinful humanity, both in His public baptism and at the Cross.[21]

5. Our conservative roots and affiliations (theological, social, political, personality).

Some avoid controversial approaches for fear of losing financial support! (The fact that many of our supporters are from conservative churches was mentioned by an administrator in connection with a policy restricting contextualisation. Could this be a sign of the beginnings of institutionalisation?) On the other hand, if we continue to commit "Christian syncretism", the modern equivalent of "Judaising the Gentiles", our churches and supporters are not going to squawk, since this is really how it has always been done. Yet it was not until the Apostle Paul risked confrontation with the established church that the will of God was made manifest to them that they should "not make it difficult for the Gentiles". Could it be that the risk of displeasing men or fear of coming under criticism or attack from Christian brothers may be freezing us up from "striving to please God" (Gal. 1:10)?

I have met those who said they want to "play it safe" by continuing with traditional approaches, rather than risk the possibility of syncretism with a contextualised approach, yet by their conservatism they actually guarantee the promulgation of "Christian" syncretism and the "anti-grace" heresy that requires Muslims to convert to another culture and communal identity. Somehow this does not concern them.

Our over-cautious conservatism hinders us from taking risks or exercising creativity for fear of being labelled radical or, worse still, heretical! (As a product of one of the bastions of orthodoxy, I have wrestled with such thoughts and concerns myself.) In treading the beaten paths of missionary method we naively think we remain solidly in the tradition of the apostles and historic Christianity. Ironically, not only is such practice contrary to the New Testament (as I have shown elsewhere), but it is contrary to the early church. The

---

[21]John D. C. Anderson, "Our Approach to Islam: Christian or Cultic?" Muslim World Pulse, 6 (Feb. 1977): p. 5.

vast majority of the Church Fathers, such as Justin, Aristides, Athenagoras, Theophilus, Clement and Origen used pagan writings to demonstrate the gospel. The British scholar, Michael Green, in his book, Evangelism in the Early Church, concludes:

Yes, the lives, the message, the deaths of Christians, showed that the risk of taking the gospel and translating it, as thoroughly as a Justin did, into other thought forms was a very worthwhile procedure. They used the Greek epics; they used the Homeric myths, and also Stoic and Epicurean philosophy when it suited them. . . . this is the characteristic aim which the Greek exponents of the gospel set themselves: to embody biblical doctrine in cultural forms which would be acceptable in their society. Not to remove the scandal of the gospel, but so to present their message in terms acceptable to their hearers, that the real scandal of the gospel could be perceived and its challenge faced. That was their aim. Many of them must have succeeded in it much of the time, or there would have been no Church strong enough to face the repeated persecutions from the state in the second and early third centuries. Often the attempt was a failure; something of the content of the message was lost with its Jewish wrappings which had been discarded. That was regrettable, but inevitable - assuming that the attempt to reach the Gentiles was worth making. And to question that is to question the universality of Christianity itself. If Christ is for all men, then evangelists must run the risk of being misunderstood, of misunderstanding elements in the gospel themselves, of losing out on the transposition of parts of the message so long as they bear witness to Him. Christians are called to live dangerously. The principle of the incarnation must be carried into Christian preaching.[22]

6. Wrong priorities and unwillingness to pay the price.

To contextualise fully requires that we pay the costly price of incarnation, imitating Christ, who did not cling to His divine prerogatives and rights, but identified with sinful humanity. For us to do the same is psychologically, spiritually and physically painful. It takes us out of our comfort zone. For example, it has much more meaning for us to pray using the forms of the Middle Eastern Protestant

---

[22]Michael Green, "Evangelism in the Early Church", p. 142. I am indebted to John Mansour for this quote, which he cites in a draft of a paper he is writing.

churches (which are the same as those in the West), than it is to use Islamic prayer forms. I once led a group of trainees in contextualised prayer adapting the Islamic ritual. The feedback from one honest participant was that he did not feel that he was really praying (but through the experience he said that he realised that a Muslim must feel the same way about the Protestant form).

It also takes a lot more time and effort to contextualise. For example, how many of us are willing to undertake prolonged study of the Qur'an and Islam in order to learn the religious vocabulary of Muslims, when we have already endured a gruelling two or more years of acquiring the ecclesiastical vocabulary of the Bible translated for the Christian minority? Likewise to contextualise theology requires study of Islamic scholarship and critical and creative thinking to formulate an indigenous theology. It is infinitely easier just to translate western theological works into a new language. Also, what about the massive effort required for a contextualised Bible translation and emotional cost of dealing with the opposition of traditionalists for doing so? Contextualisation is the hard path - as was the cross!

7. Ignorance of the degree to which western Christianity has been contextualised.

It may be instructive for those of us from the West to recognise some of the areas in which contextualisation occurred in the transmission and development of the message within western cultures. The Easter message, for example, is the foundation and essence of our faith. Yet Easter was the Teutonic spring goddess of fertility. The new plant life of this pagan belief was appropriated as a useful symbol of the new life Christians experience through Christ. Then we have the western observance on Dec. 25 of Christmas, which is the result of contextualised ministry and accommodation to local custom, not historical fact. Romans gave gifts on Dec. 25 long before Christ was born. Further examples are Christmas trees, which were of pagan origin; Halloween was transformed into All Saints' Night and what about Martin Luther's appropriation of German beer drinking songs for the tunes of some of our great hymns? What about the way we pray with our hands folded? Missionaries taught converts from the warlike German peoples to pray (innovating a new form) to express the "binding" of their hands from war in submission to the teaching of Christ.

8. Lack of leadership, pioneers and modelling

In closing, I must acknowledge my belief that there are many workers who are open to or desirous of contextualising their ministries, but are not able to pull it off themselves. Many need a leader to follow in this endeavour - a pioneer to blaze the trail before them. Others lack a Jonathan whom they can assist like an armour-bearer. Perhaps most merely await the impetus of their team to agree to commit themselves to the task, plan how to tackle it and organise to accomplish it. The need is for leadership both stateside and on the field. Leaders who feel the burden of this vision must pray, initiate and facilitate this work, as well as encourage and support practitioners who innovate, experiment and develop new models. Without leadership contextualisation will remain but a policy on paper, and that leadership must provide an atmosphere of trust and freedom, or there will be no creativity, innovation or progress.

Conclusion

Many factors undoubtedly influence one's stand regarding contextualisation. This paper has proposed some of the factors which I believe reduce our proper interest and commitment to its implementation. I hope that each reader will evaluate himself and those around him in light of the factors mentioned, and see if there be need for change. If there is, then may we not rest until we have done what needs to be done!

True Islam?
By N.F.

1. What does true Islam mean?

The word Islam is one of the words in today's world which creates different feelings amongst different people according to how they may take it. To understand the meaning of the word, we have to go to the Qur'an for clarification:

Sura 3:85 *If anyone desires a religion other than Islam (submission to Allah), never will it be accepted of him; and in the*

Hereafter he will be in the ranks of those who have lost (all spiritual good).

Sura 5:4 *This day have those who reject Faith given up all hope of your religion: Yet fear them not but fear Me. This day have I perfected your religion for you, completed My favour upon you, and have chosen for you Islam as your religion. But if any is forced by hunger, with no inclination to transgression, Allah is indeed Oft-Forgiving, Most Merciful. See also Sura 3:19 and 20*

- Does Islam mean to follow the prophet Mohammed (p.b.u.h) and practise the five pillars?

- Does the word 'Muslim' only refer to the followers of the prophet Mohammed (p.b.u.h)?

- Did Islam begin with the prophet Mohammed (p.b.u.h)?

To get answers for these questions, let us start with the definition of Islam.

Islam: Is the total submission of one's will to Allah, or an act of resignation to His will, and the Arabic root of the word Islam means 'act of resignation'.

The prophets before the prophet Mohammed (p.b.u.h) were Muslims:

Sura 22:78 *And strive in His cause as ye ought to strive, (with sincerity and under discipline). He has chosen you, and has imposed no difficulties on you in religion; it is the cult of your father Abraham. It is He Who has named you Muslims, both **before** and in this (The Qur'an); that the Apostle may be a witness for you, and ye be a witness for mankind! So establish regular Prayer, give regular Charity, and hold fast to Allah! He is your Protector—the best to protect and the Best to help!*

Sura 5:47 *It was We (Allah) who revealed the Law (to Moses): Therein was guidance and light. By its standard have been judged the Jews, **by the Prophets who bowed (as in Islam) to Allah's Will, by the Rabbis and the Doctors of Law:** For to them was entrusted the protection of Allah's Book, and they were witnesses thereto: Therefore fear not men, but fear Me, and sell not My signs for a miserable price. If any do fail to judge by* *(the light of) what Allah hath revealed, they are (no better than) Unbelievers.*

Did they follow the prophet Mohammed (p.b.u.h) or practise the five pillars?

Abraham was a Muslim:

Sura 3:76 *Abraham was not a Jew nor yet a Christian; but he was upright and bowed his will to Allah's (which is Islam). And joined not gods with Allah.*

Did he follow the prophet Mohammed (p.b.u.h) or practise the five pillars?

The disciples of Jesus were Muslims:

Sura 3:52 *When Jesus found unbelief on their part He said: "Who will be my helpers to (the work of) Allah?" Said the Disciples: "We are Allah's helpers: We believe in Allah and do thou bear witness that **we are Muslims.**"*

Did they follow the prophet Mohammed (p.b.u.h) or practise the five pillars?

Islam is submission to Allah not particularly following the prophet Mohammed and practising the five pillars, what is interesting is that this meaning of Submission to God is not only found but originated the Old and New Testaments of the Bible:

Exodus 20:1 *And God spake all these words, saying, 2 I am the LORD thy God, which have brought thee out of the land of Egypt, out of the house of bondage. 3 Thou **shalt have no other gods** before me. 4 Thou shalt not make unto thee any graven image, or any likeness of any thing that is in heaven above, or that is in the earth beneath, or that is in the water under the earth: 5 Thou **shalt not bow down** thyself to them, nor serve them: for I the LORD thy God am a jealous God, visiting the iniquity of the fathers upon the children unto the third and fourth generation of them that hate me; 6 And **showing** mercy unto thousands of them that love me, and keep my commandments. See also Genesis 12:1-4 and Genesis 22.*

Matthew 7:21 *Not every one that saith unto me, Lord, Lord, shall enter into the kingdom of heaven; but he that doeth **the will** of my Father which is in heaven.*

John 5:30 *I can of mine own self do nothing: as I hear, I judge: and my judgement is just; because I seek not mine own will, but **the will** of the Father which hath sent me.*

James 4:7 **Submit yourselves,** *then, to God,* see also Romans 10:3.

So the true meaning of Islam as submission to Allah, is a universal message which is found not only in the Qu'ran, but originated from the Bible in the first place. Moreover, every person must be Muslim (submit to Allah)!

2. Man disobeyed and rebelled against Allah the creator!

The human soul is prone to evil. Adam is an example of the human being who broke away and did not submit to Allah. He who was created by Allah and created to worship Allah and live in obedience to the Most Holy One, rebelled against his Creator.

Sura 20:123 *He said: "Get ye down, both of you, —all together, from the Garden, with enmity one to another: But if, as is sure, there comes to you guidance from Me, whosoever follows My guidance, will not lose his way, nor fall into misery.*

Man (everyone on earth) does not want to follow real Islam by submitting to Allah:

Sura 16:61 *If Allah were to punish men for their wrongdoing, **He would not leave, (on the earth), a single living creature:** But He gives them respite for a stated Term: When their Term expires, they would not be able to delay (the punishment) for a single hour, just as they would not be able to anticipate it (for a single hour).*

Sura 12:53 *"Nor do I absolve my own self (of blame): **The (human) soul is certainly prone to evil,***

Sura 19:71,72 **Not one** *of you but will pass over it **(hill):** This is, with thy Lord, **a Decree which must be accomplished.** 72 But We shall save those who guarded against evil, and We shall leave **the wrong doers** therein, (Humbled) to their knees.*

3. Man needs Allah's Mercy:

Sura 12:53 *"**unless my Lord do bestow His Mercy**: But surely my Lord is Oft-Forgiving, Most Merciful."*

THEREFORE:

As everyone on this earth is a wrong doer (Sura 16:61), Man must be true Muslim (submits to Allah) by accepting **His Mercy** to be from those who guarded against evil (Those who accept Allah's Mercy and Guidance.)

BUT

As submission to Allah is not a choice, but a need for all, humans are prone to evil unless they are saved through His Mercy. So, the only way for submission to take place is through **Allah's Mercy.**

Unfortunately people can not be saved by doing good deeds.

Sura 40:16 *The Day whereon they will (all) come forth: Not a single thing concerning them is hidden from Allah. Whose will be the Dominion that Day? That of Allah, the One, the Irresistible!*

The question can then be asked how people can be saved if Allah knows all the sins of each person?

The Qur'an gives a clear answer to this question:

Sura 47:19 *Know, therefore, that there is no god but Allah, and* **ask forgiveness for thy fault,** *and for the men and women who believe: For Allah knows how ye move about and how ye dwell in your homes.*

Sura 48:2 ***That Allah may forgive thee thy faults of the past and those to follow;*** *fulfil His favour to thee; and guide thee on the Straight Way; 3 And that **Allah may help thee with powerful help.***

Yes, Allah wants to forgive! He is full of Mercy and Kindness! Every person needs this Mercy. Even the prophet Mohammed (p.b.u.h) needed Allah's Mercy - Bukhari VOL VIII 81- the book of Ar-riqaq, Chapter 18: 6463; 6464; 6467. *Narrated Abu Huraira: Allah's apostle said: "The deeds of **any one** of you **will not save you** (from the fire)." They said, "**Even you (will not be saved by your deeds), O Allah's apostle?**" He said, "**No, even I** (will not be saved by my deeds) **unless and until** Allah bestows **His mercy** on me."*

Sura 11: 90 *"But ask forgiveness of your Lord, and turn unto Him (in repentance): For my Lord is indeed full of mercy and loving kindness."*

4. Who is Allah's Mercy?

Sura 19: 20,21 *She said: "How shall I have a son, seeing that no man has touched me, and I am not Unchaste?" 21 He said: "So (it will be): Thy Lord saith, 'That is easy for Me: And (We wish) to appoint him as a Sign unto men and a Mercy from Us': It is a matter (so) decreed."*

5. How Jesus is Allah's Mercy?

The story of Abraham explains to us how Jesus is Allah's Mercy. We read about the sacrifice of Abraham's son:

Sura 37:107 *And We (Allah)* **ransomed** *him with a* **momentous sacrifice**:

The sacrifice of the lamb which Allah has given so that Abraham's son could live, does not equal the life of Abraham's son. It was a symbolic sign to a greater Sacrifice, Just as the lamb was given to save Abraham's son, so Jesus is Allah's Lamb to save people from their sin. John 1:29 *"The next day John saw Jesus coming toward him and said: 'Look, the* **Lamb of God**, *who takes away the sin of the world!'"*

-How can this be?

Jesus had no human father. He was sent from Allah to sacrifice the human soul. He is a momentous sacrifice as he was sent from Allah. Jesus has one message- that He came to die as a momentous sacrifice for those prone to evil. This is how Jesus is a Mercy from Allah. Allah sent His Mercy to save those guarded against evil, involved Jesus dying on the cross as a momentous sacrifice. Acceptance of Allah's Mercy (Of Jesus dying on the cross to buy us back, to ransom us) is necessary for our salvation.

He is a Pure Son (**has no soul incites evil**) sent from Allah:

Sura 19:19 He said: "Nay, I am only a messenger from thy Lord, (to announce) to thee the gift of **a holy son**."

Jesus is the Word of Allah to communicate through him His Mercy:

Sura 3:45 Behold! The angels said: "O Mary! Allah giveth thee glad tidings of **a Word from Him:** His name will be Christ Jesus, the son of Mary, **held in honour in this world and the Hereafter** and of (the company of) those **nearest to Allah;"**

The Qur'an confirms the death of Jesus!

I. The death of Jesus on the cross

Sura 4:157,158 *That **they** said (in boast), "**We** killed Christ Jesus the son of Mary, the Apostle of Allah"; —But **they** killed him not, nor crucified him, but so it was made to appear to **them**, and those who differ therein are full of doubts, with no (certain) knowledge, but only conjecture to follow, for of a surety **they** killed him not: 158 Nay, Allah raised him up unto Himself; and Allah is Exalted in Power, Wise.*

In these verses the subject is the Jews not Jesus! The first verse does not say Jesus not killed, it says the Jews did not kill him:

1) It was actually the Romans who killed/crucified Jesus.

2) It was not the Jews who slew Jesus. Allah allowed it to confer a benefit. As in Sura 8:17 *It is **not ye** who **slew them**; it was **Allah:** When thou threwest (a handful of dust), it was not thy act, but Allah's: In order that He might test the Believers by a gracious trial from Himself: For Allah is He Who heareth and knoweth (all things).*

3) Those who are slain in Allah's way are not to be thought of as dead — for they live. As in Sura 3:169 *Think not of those who are **slain in Allah's way** as **dead.** Nay, **they live**, finding their sustenance in the Presence of their Lord.*

In the second verse Allah raised Jesus up unto Himself, elsewhere Sura 19:33 *"So Peace is on me the day I was **born**, the day that **I die**, and the day that I shall be **raised up to life** (again)"* we see a Sequence of Jesus' death is followed by Allah raising him up. Sura 3:55 *"Behold! Allah said: "O Jesus! I will **take thee (cause you to die)** and **raise thee** to Myself and clear thee (of the falsehoods) of those who blaspheme; I will make those who follow thee* *superior to those who reject faith, to the Day of Resurrection: Then shall ye all return unto me, and I will judge between you of the matters wherein ye dispute."*

Word study on 'take' = death:

1) Sura 4:15 *"If any of your women are guilty of lewdness, take the evidence of four (reliable) witnesses from amongst you against them; and if they testify, confine them to houses until **death** do claim them, or Allah ordain for them some (other) way."*

2) Sura 32:11 *Say: "The Angel of Death, put in charge of you, will (duly) **take your souls**: Then shall ye be brought back to your Lord."*

3) Sura 2:234 *If any of you **die** and leave widows behind, they shall wait concerning themselves four months and ten days: When they have fulfilled their term, there is no blame on you if they dispose of themselves in a just and reasonable manner. And Allah is well acquainted with what ye do.*

4) Sura 2:240 *Those of you who **die** and leave widows should bequeath for their widows a year's maintenance and residence; but if they leave (the residence), there is no blame on you for what they do with themselves, provided it is reasonable. And Allah is Exalted in Power, Wise.*

5) Sura 12:101 *"O my Lord! Thou hast indeed bestowed on me some power, and taught me something of the interpretation of dreams and events, —O Thou Creator of the heavens and the earth! Thou art my Protector in this world and in the Hereafter. **Take Thou my soul** (at death) as one submitting to thy Will (as a Muslim), and unite me with the righteous."*

II. Two categories of prophets

A. 1) those who were called imposters

   2) those who were slain

Sura 5:70 *We took the Covenant of the Children of Israel and sent them apostles. Every time there came to them an apostle with what they themselves desired not—some (of these) **they called imposters**, and some **they (go so far as to) slay**.*

B. Allah gave:

1) Moses and the apostles (The Book).

2) Jesus (clear signs and strengthened him with the holy spirit).

Sura 2:87 *We gave **Moses the Book** and followed him up with a succession of **Apostles;** We gave **Jesus** the son of Mary **Clear (Signs) and strengthened him with the Holy Spirit.** Is it that whenever there comes to you an Apostle with what ye yourselves desire not, ye are puffed up with pride? —Some ye call **impostors,** and others ye slay!*

1) Moses and the apostles (The Book) .... some 1) they called impostors.

2)Jesus (Clear signs and strengthened with the holy spirit) .... some 2) they slew.

III. Jesus was given clear signs: Sura 3:183 *They (also) said: "Allah took our promise not to believe in an apostle unless he showed us a sacrifice consumed by fire (from heaven)." Say: "There came to you apostles before me, with **Clear Signs** and even with what ye ask for: Why then did ye **slay** them, if ye speak the truth?"*

IV. Allah enjoined on Jesus prayer and zakat as long as he lives: Sura 19:31 *"And He hath made me blessed wheresoever I be, and hath enjoined on me **Prayer** and **Charity** as long as I live.*

Q/ If Jesus never died and Allah raised him alive, what kind of charity and to whom did he give? Are there poor in heaven? The only way that Jesus is freed from the enjoinment of charity is by death.

Conclusion: From all the verses above that talks about Jesus' death, we can see that the Qur'an confirms the death of Jesus as Allah's Mercy and sacrifice (*a Sign unto men and a Mercy from Us': It is a matter (so) decreed.* 19:21) to ransom Man from punishment for the wrongdoings they commit (*a Decree which must be accomplished.* 19:71)

6. How can we experience forgiveness?

By accepting Jesus as Allah's sacrifice, we accept Allah's Mercy and will receive forgiveness of our sins:

Sura 16: 61 *If Allah were to punish men for their wrongdoing, He would not leave, on the (earth), a single living creature*: But He gives them respite for a stated Term: When their Term expires, they would not be able to delay (the punishment) for a single hour, just as they would not be able to anticipate it (for a single hour).

Sura 12: 53 "Nor do I absolve my own self (of blame): The (human) soul is certainly prone to evil, *unless my Lord do bestow His Mercy*: But surely my Lord is Oft-Forgiving, Most Merciful."

Jesus' sacrifice can forgive sins because He is Allah's Mercy and He is the Straight Way which leads The human soul away from being prone to evil back to submission to Allah (True Islam). The only one message of Allah to Man:

The Qur'an confirms Jesus is The Straight Way!

Sura 1: 6 *Show us the straight way,* 7 *The way of those on whom Thou hast bestowed Thy Grace, Those whose (portion) is not wrath, and who go not astray.*

Sura 43: 61 *And (Jesus) shall be a Sign (for the coming) of the Hour (of Judgment): Therefore have no doubt about the Hour, but follow ye Me: This is a Straight Way.*

Sura 43: 63 *When Jesus came with Clear Signs, he said: "Now have I come to you with Wisdom, and in order to make clear to you some of the (points) on which ye dispute: Therefore fear Allah and obey me. 64 "For Allah, He is my Lord and your Lord: So worship ye Him: This is a Straight Way."*

Sura 36: 61 *"And that ye should Worship Me, (for that) this was the Straight Way."*

Therefore following Jesus and Obeying his teachings (accepting and believing in him and his demonstration as Allah's Sacrifice and Mercy) is the straight way that leads to worship and submission to Allah in true Islam.

7. The only message of Allah to humanity:

Submission to Allah the most Holy and Forgiving One, means to follow the Straight Way, obey Jesus who has given His Life as Allah's Mercy and through Whom (Allah's mercy) we can experience One's forgiveness!

True Islam means to submit to Allah, by accepting and following Jesus, the Straight Way, and accept His Mercy "the sacrifice" of Jesus on the cross!

APPENDIX A
Culture's Consequences

The following material has largely been taken from Hofstede's book, 'Culture's Consequences'[1]. I include it because the conclusions of his research are so important in understanding and approaching missions and a reasonable strategy in cross-cultural thinking. I have been greatly helped in finding his work so applicable to our situation and what was in a way intuitive now has some rational and logical apologetic for it.

This section attempts to highlight some of the thinking behind the *'near neighbour'* concept, as discussed so far. Understanding the cultural differences between sending and receiving cultures will be the difference between breakthrough and deadlock.

Between 1966 and 1978 Geert Hofstede carried out research for the Hermes corporation. This research was aimed at trying to understand the elements of culture that governed the lives and style of managers. The results have major implications for the church, missions and world evangelism in general.

Culture is the personality of the group. It stabilises under a number of forces such as nature, man himself, his interaction with other men, trade and conquest. All of these elements force and stabilise change. Modern advancing technology brings about even swifter change; just witness the emergence of the global village catalysed by the Internet.

Man responds to these forces by developing norms of acceptable behaviour and associated values systems. This leads to the development of structures and institutions which constantly reinforce these norms, see Figure 1.

---

1 References & page numbers quoted are from; Hofstede, Geert. 1984 Culture's Consequences - International Differences in Work Related Values (Abridged Edition). SAGE Publications Ltd. ISBN 0-8039-1306-0

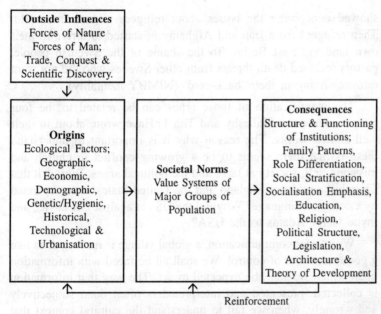

Figure 1: The Stabilising of Culture Patterns

All cultures can be broken down into a number of constituent elements or aspects (as Hofstede defined). The relative mixture of these aspects, both individually and collectively, helps to define a particular culture's characteristics. These comments and his research allow for the fact that there will be people within each culture that do not fit the norm. This is not to disqualify the norm but in fact highlights it.

The Four Aspects of Culture;

1) Power distance or respect (PD)
2) Uncertainty avoidance (UA)
3) Individualism versus Collectivism (IDV)
4) Male / Female (Masc)

There are national or racial traits, as well as personal traits, within a given race. For example, although Americans rate high on the individualism scale, some break with the norm and exhibit strong communal characteristics. However, it is seen that in a crisis, where pre-condition is the fallback position, most revert to the national type. I remember being impressed by the caring concern that Swedes showed concerning the issues about refugees around the world. Then refugees from Iran and Afghanistan started to arrive in their own land via East Berlin. To the shame of the Swedish people, pastors received death threats from other Swedes who did not want refugees living in their 'back-yard' (NIMBY mentality).

The identification of those types can be related to the four temperaments that Hallesby and Tim LaHaye wrote about in their well-known works. The reason why it is important to understand these is that there seems to be a growing conflict in church and missions, self, society at large and the political arena. Why is it that Churchill could say England and the United States were separated by a common language? Why did the US act against UK advice and invite Gerry Adams to the USA?

With faster communication, a global village is rushing at us like a goods train out of control. We shall all be faced with information upon which we shall be expected to act. The way that information is collected, presented and interpreted is often done subjectively and wrongly, when we fail to understand the cultural context that the presenter is coming from.

Certain denominations have arisen and thrived, as form and structures have attracted certain cultural types. For example, the Brethren movement is an individualistic, low power distance, masculine one, whereas the Anglican church is a high power distance, female community (generally speaking).

Possibly because of the barren and short growing season in Scandinavia, the populace couldn't produce sufficient food. Consequently Vikings took to raiding the UK from across the seas. This left the women to run the family, the home and the food resources. This produced a coping female culture, which could still change characteristics given further influences.

Power Distance

Definition: PD, is concerned with the concentration of power and the exercise of it over subordinates. It measures interpersonal power.

Individualism

Definition: IDV, the relationship between the individual and the collective whole.

Male/female

Definition: Masc, looks at the sex characteristics role in societies and organisations.

Uncertainty Avoidance

Definition: UA, is the degree by which people can live with uncertainty, defined in following rules, employment stability and stress.

It has been shown that PD and IDV are directly related. This is graphically shown in fig 1.1. Hofstede found no case where small PD (USA, CAN, GB, NZ, NL i.e. Protestant, wealthy countries) and collectivism go together. This seems to suggest that Protestantism, free market economics, and individualism go together. On reflection one would expect an environment where individuals are encouraged to maximise their potential which would produce a wealthy economy. On the other hand Catholic lands score low in Individualism but high in PD.

Why has this division come about? How have these national characteristics emerged? Hofstede suggests that the dividing line can be traced geographically through Northern Europe, the southern States being Catholic and having the papal system as a model for all institutions. The Germanic countries were not under the Pope but were tribal in nature. Tribalism relied on a council of tribal elders, accessibility to the leadership and consensus, which values the individual's opinion.

This set the cultural pattern in North & South Europe and the revolution led by Luther in the Protest, which could be seen as an overthrow of a PD culture dressed up in theological terms, or it could be seen as an emergence of an alternative "tribal" culture, based upon biblical study (Israel and 12 tribes) and in contrast to the Papal high PD culture.

Certainly Jesus operated on a low PD in that He was accessible to the people and His 'subordinates' to the point of calling them brethren. It was recognised that He had power and authority but that it was given to Him by God (and to His followers, in that they gladly received Him).

It is interesting therefore that recent missions have come from the Protestant countries with Britain leading the way, along with

Holland in the 19th century and the US in the second half of the 20th century. I now understand why Malta would not allow Catholic priests that came from Protestant countries on to the island. The possible danger was that Protestant cultural values would be imparted by those priests, albeit unwittingly.

The missionaries who got down to the people were hugely individualistic and pioneered modern mission. This was not without problems and that is the point of this paper. The Protestant, Northern European, Germanic culture is usually in conflict with, and destructive of, Asian, African, and Latin American cultures. These tend to be high PD, low individualism, female and high in uncertainty avoidance.

The next (and possibly final) phase of world mission may well have to be carried out by those coming from a non-Protestant culture, because the vast number of people yet to be reached come from cultures similar to those of non-Protestant lands.

I Power Distance

LOW PD cultures seek for equality whilst never actually achieving it. Mulder (p. 71) describes the characteristics of PD.

- The mere exercise of power will give satisfaction.

- The more powerful individual will strive to maintain or to increase the power distance to the less powerful person.

- The greater this distance from the less powerful person, the stronger the striving to increase it.

- Individuals will strive to reduce the power distance between themselves and more powerful persons.

- The smaller this distance from the more powerful person, the stronger the tendency to reduce it.

It is interesting that danger of conflict does not come in the early stages of an organisation's development but much later. Power striving by subordinates does not come from dissatisfaction but by satisfaction. Delegating power to subordinates feeds a need to get more and thus an attempt to overthrow the leader comes about after some time in the organisation. Loyalty, humility and Christian love should not lead to a struggle for power but

Position	Country PD Index	Position	Country PD Index
1	Malayasia	27/28	South Korea
2/3	Guatemala	29/30	Iran
2/3	Panama	29/30	Taiwan
4	Philippines	31	Spain
5/6	Mexico	32	Pakistan
5/6	Venezuela	33	Japan
7	Arab Countires	34	Italy
8/9	Ecuador	35/36	South Africa
8/9	Indonesia	37	Jamaica
10/11	India	38	USA
10/11	West Africa	39	Canada
12	Yugoslavia	40	Netherlands
13	Singapore	41	Australia
14	Brazil	42/44	Costa Rica
15/16	France	42/44	Germany
15/16	Hong Kong	42/44	Great Britain
17	Colombia	45	Switzerland
18/19	El Salvador	46	Finland
20	Belgium	47/48	Norway
21/23	East Africa	47/48	Sweden
21/23	Peru	49	Eire
21/23	Thailand	50	New Zealand
24/25	Portugal	51	Denmark
26	Uruguay	52	Israel
27/28	Greece	53	Austria

Figure 2: Country Index of Power Distance

Christians are also human and this kind of struggle can be even more bitter, being couched in spiritual and biblical terminology by the rebellious.

There will be a struggle by leaders to maintain their PD from subordinates whilst subordinates will try to reduce the power between themselves and their leader. Thus many conflicts in church and mission organisations can be attributed to this clash of culture. Protestant lands like England, Scotland and Northern Ireland will always be in conflict with more culturally Catholic lands like Wales, France, Spain and Eire, which are Papal or Celtic in culture. The conflict in Northern Ireland can be seen in the light of this clash of cultures.

Thus PD can be shown to be supported by a national culture, although there will be some who break the mould, but they will be a minority.

I was with a group of Korean pastors recently and I was treated as the honoured guest. The first question asked was "How old are you?" In Korean society (and the church) the "pecking order" is established by age status which establishes the PD. Any Korean working within a US or UK organisation will find great cultural adjustment which, if maintained over a period long enough will spoil them and frustrate them on re-entering a high PD culture like Korea. By the way, my response to "How old are you?" was 107 years. This brought a round of laughter, as they realised what they were attempting to do. The national cultural characteristics will spill over from one sphere of life into another. It helps us to find a place within each activity and know how to relate. Those not knowing the culture will either clash with members in that society or can act as a listening ear to complaints and hurts, because they are seen to be outside the structure. An American pastor in an English church can be seen as not fitting (by virtue that his accent is not classified) into a working or any other class and thus can easily relate to his congregation over a range of classes. Most churches reflect a class structure and people move in or out of church because they either fit or do not fit into the prevailing culture. Even theological positions and biblical interpretations can be seen as a response to cultural "glasses". Characteristics of PD can be seen in Figure 3.

II Individualism *(See Figure 4)*

Allied to, yet distinct from, PD is the concept of individualism. It reflects the way people live together, whether as a communal whole or whether they see themselves as individuals. Americans, Australians, NZ are classic examples of individualists, probably forced by the need to pioneer and settle huge territories to rely upon themselves against the elements and hostile environment. The Vikings also were pioneers, but went as teams or crews in their long boats from a given village to explore, exploit and range over the seas. They came second as a Scandinavian group behind these others as individualists. Catholic countries score lower down, as do Muslim and Asian groups.

Consequences for Political Systems

Low PD	High PD
• Pluralist governments based on outcome of majority votes	• Autocratic or oligarchic governments
• No sudden changes in forms of government (evolution and stability)	• Sudden changes in form of government (revolution and/or instability)
• Political parties exist and tend to be in the centre with relatively weak left and right wings	• If political parties exist, there is a polarisation between left and right with a weak centre
• Government is frequently led by parties stressing equality, usually social democrats	• If government is based on election results, it tends to be led by parties not stressing equality (right wing)
• Tax system aims at redistributing wealth	• Tax system protects the wealthy
• Free labour unions exist and tend to be pragmatically orientated	• If free labour unions exist, these tend to be ideologically based and involved in politics

Consequences for Religious Life, Philosophical and Ideological Thinking

Low PD	High PD
• Success of religions stressing equality	• Success of religions stressing stratification
• Ideologies of power equalisation	• Ideologies of power polarisation
• Pluralist theorists about society	• Elitist theories about society
• Non-zero-sum theories of power	• Zero-sum theories of power
• 'Foxes' approach is seen as leading to stability	• 'Lions' approach is seen as leading to stability
• More, Marx, Weber, Mulder, Tannenbaum	• Machiavelli, Mosca, Pareto, Michels

Consequences for Organisations

Low PD	High PD
• Less centralisation	• Greater centralisation
• Flatter organisation pyramids	• Tall organisation pyramids
• Smaller proportion of supervisory personnel	• Large proportion of supervisory personnel
• Smaller wage differentials	• Large wage differentials
• High qualification of lower strata	• Low qualification of lower strata
• Manual work same status as clerical work	• White-collar jobs valued more than blue-collar jobs

Figure 3: Consequences of National Power Distance Index Differences

Country	IDV Index	Country	IDV Index
1	USA	26/27	Arab countries
2	Australia	28	Turkey
3	Great Britain	29	Uruguay
4/5	Canada	30	Greece
4/5	Netherlands	31	Philippines
6	New Zealand	32	Mexico
7	Italy	33/35	East Africa
8	Belgium	33/35	Yugoslavia
9	Denmark	33/35	Portugal
10/11	Sweden	36	Malaysia
10/11	France	37	Hong Kong
12	Eire	38	Chile
13	Norway	39/41	West Africa
14	Switzerland	39/41	Singpoare
15	Germany	39/41	Thailand
16	South Africa	42	El Salvador
17	Finland	43	South Korea
18	Austria	44	Taiwan
19	Israel	45	Peru
20	Spain	46	Costa Rica
21	India	47/48	Pakistan
22/23	Japan	47/48	Indonesia
22/23	Argentina	49	Colombia
23	Iran	50	Venezuela
25	Jamaica	51	Panama
26/27	Brazil	52	Ecuador
		53	Guatemala

Figure 4: Country Index of Individualism

Belgium, France and Italy all rank higher than the rest, although they also have a lower PD than Protestant lands.

Some animals hunt in packs, like the dog or lion, others singly, as the tiger. Man shows differing attitudes to this gregarious nature he is assumed to have. There is a variety of types of family units that can be a mix from husband, wife, child to the extended family or tribal unit based upon kinship. Hunting communities tend to live in nuclear families whilst agriculturists build cities, develop crafts associated with harvests and grow into kinship structures.

If one in this extended family or tribe breaks ranks culturally, there are sanctions that can be applied, up to death. We find this in Islam, which codified a most common human practice in order to preserve the newly emerging Islamic tribe after Muhammad's death. To this day a Muslim faces the most severe sanctions if he changes his religion. One can choose to join the Islamic Umma or community but never to leave it.

No wonder missionaries coming from a highly individualistic culture like US, UK, NZ or Australia find it difficult to understand Muslim communities or to penetrate them with any success. The people who are "successful" in Muslim evangelism are those who come from a similar culture to the Muslim.

This individualism affects not only the way we live together but also mental programming, the structure of our institutions, the form the church takes, our attitude to education and family life. It has been very popular to promote team-work for missionaries in Muslim lands, in order that they may survive. This "team-work" is actually self- defeating, since it allows for the perpetuation of a western culture within an Islamic country and so the missionary never becomes acclimatised and integrated in order to become "...all things to all people in order to win some" 1Cor 9[19-22]. The central element in our mental programming or world view is the view we have of ourselves. Traditional or community thinkers hardly ever think of themselves. Thus being asked to decide for Christ (or whatever jargon is used by that denomination) their first thought is: "What would my father say, how would the elders react, shall I bring shame on the mother that bore and suckled me?"

The western concept of personality does not even exist in Chinese thinking. We see ourselves as being distinct from society, the Chinese do not. This concept is me and my society, thus HK, Taiwan and Singapore score low on the ID table. Historically all movements have been based upon a family or community being converted e.g. Acts 16[33]. Father Donovan in his book Christianity Rediscovered tells of his fruitless work amongst Masai people until he became a nomad with them. He would ask for a meeting with the tribal leaders, present the church teachings to them then return months later to see if the tribe wanted to convert. Many did, some did not and he did not bother them after that.

Low IDV	High IDV
• In society people are born into extended families or clans which protect them in exchange for loyalty	• In society everyone is supposed to take care of him- or herself and his or her immediate family
• 'We' consciousness	• 'I' consciousness
• Collectivity-orientation	• Self orientation
• Identity is based in the social system	• Identity is based in the individual
• Emotional dependence of individual on organisations and institutions.	• Emotional independence of individual from organisations or institutions
• Emphasis on belonging to an organisation; membership ideal	• Emphasis on individual initiative and achievement; leadership ideal
• Private life is invaded by organisations and clans to which one belongs; opinions are predetermined.	• Everyone has a right to a private life and opinion
• Expertise, order, duty, security provided by organisation or clan	• Autonomy, variety, pleasure, individual financial security
• Friendships predetermined by stable social relationships; but need for prestige within these relationships	• Need for specific friendships
• Belief in group decisions	• Belief in individual decisions
• Value standards differ for in-groups and out-groups; particularism	• Value standards should apply to universalism

Figure 5: The Individualism Societal Norm

Americans see their individualism as contributing to the greatness of the US. Each is guided by an inner gyroscope, the 'force with them' having no community based mentality or guidance system. Now the TV film and pop star has become the guide for this generation.

Low IDV Countries	High IDV Countries
• Importance of provisions by company (training, physical conditions)	• Importance of employees' personal life (time)
• Emotional dependence on company	• Emotional independence of company
• Large company attractive	• Small company attractive
• Moral involvement with company	• Calculative involvement with company

Low IDV Countries	High IDV Countries
• More importance attached to training and use of skills in jobs	• More importance attached to freedom and challenge in jobs
• Students consider it less socially acceptable to claim pursuing their own ends without minding others	• Students consider it socially acceptable to claim pursuing their own ends without minding others
• Managers aspire to conformity and orderliness	• Managers aspire to leadership and variety
• Managers rate having security in their position more important	• Managers rate having autonomy more important
• Managers endorse 'traditional' points of view, not supporting employee initiative and group activity questions	• Managers endorse 'modern' points of view on stimulating employee initiative and group activity
• Group decisions are considered better than individual decisions	• However, individual decisions are considered better than group decisions
• Duty in life appeals to students	• Enjoyment in life appeals to students
• Managers choose duty, expertness and prestige as life goals	• Managers choose pleasure, affection and security as life goals
• Individual initiative is socially frowned upon; fatalism	• Individual initiative is socially encouraged
• More acquiescence in responses to 'importance' questions	• Less acquiescence in responses to 'importance' questions
• People thought of as in-groups and out-groups; particularism	• People thought of in general terms; universalism
• Social relations predetermined in terms of in-groups	• Need to make specific friendships
• More years of schooling needed to do a given job	• Fewer years of schooling needed to do a given job
• More traffic accidents per 1000 vehicles	• Fewer traffic accidents per 1000 vehicles
• More traditional time use pattern	• More modern time use pattern

Figure 6: Summary of Implications for Individualism Index Differences

To the Asian, individualism is selfish, evil, destructive. Iran sees America as the great Satan for this very reason. Mao Tse Tung's communist philosophy came directly out of his Chinese culture. Communism was a veneer over a cultural nationalism that possibly he did not even recognise. That is the danger in this issue of conflicting ideologies. Their roots and origins, motivation and power lie deep in the individual and national conscious, not in reason or truth. There is, of course, a middle ground steered through these seeming contradictions of the alienation of privatisation and a tyranny of the collective mind. I remember meeting an intelligent Egyptian in a park in Madrid who had run away from home and his "domineering" parents on the advice of his psychiatrist. He wanted to pursue his love of languages, whilst his parents insisted he become a doctor. The tension had almost destroyed him. The contrast to this is that streets in the UK are filled with men and women whose parents had showed no interest in them at all.

When I lived in Iran, my landlord had 3 children. One he sent to a French Catholic school, one to an American Presbyterian school and the last to a mosque school. The father used his children as a political tool in case one day he might need help from any one of the power sources. The day came when there was an Islamic revolution and he had built up friends in that quarter; the family was preserved.

It is the axis of individualism versus collectivism which seems to relate most directly to a country's economic level. The most developed nations and the 'tiger' economies are all individualistic to some degree. The Asian economies are being fuelled and led by Chinese entrepreneurial genius.

It has been the USA that has exported this new individualism, but it has been widely adapted as the recipient nations (cultures) have allowed their own cultures to adapt to the new thinking.

This individualism is reflected in the kind of work goals that people have. High on the list, in a positive way, are personal time, freedom, challenge. In a negative way the organisation is supposed to do certain things for the individual: provide training, supply good work conditions, allow the use of skills.

Western missions, of course, attract individualistic people because they have so many 'mountains' to climb to get to the field. However, they are not intrinsically the best kind of people to do the work. Better to recruit workers from the closest possible culture to the target people, so that there is a minimum of disturbance of the culture and a maximum identification with the people.

IDV correlates very closely with PD. In figure 1.1 there are groups that show this ideal scenario for recruitment. Turks relate well within Brazilian culture, Singapore with Thai. All Muslim countries are well down in the IDV scale, as are Philippines, Mexico, Singapore and Latin America. Maybe these are or will be the key countries to finish the task of world evangelism.

Interestingly enough, high IDV cultures also produce fewer traffic accidents; this is possibly attributable to a higher personal responsibility, a calculative approach to life in general and a high regard for the law. Muslim countries have low IDV, high PD, reflecting that view of God who is distant and all-powerful, leading to fatalism and high traffic accidents. When I fly, I have noticed that Middle Eastern airline stewards only rarely check that my seat belt is secure on take off. This confirms the possibility of lack of general responsibility.

Low IDV cultures have a greater dependence upon the organisation and expect it to provide all their needs. High IDV culture organisations tend to allow freedom and not provide detailed instructions. Greek culture fits firmly in the Asian model along with Turkey and Brazil. It is also the highest on the UA scale and we should expect to find these characteristics in Fig 4.1, which includes worry about the future, resistance to change, gerontocracy, that managers should be chosen on the basis of age not ability, fear of failure, lacking in risk-taking over preoccupation with need for instructions, no compromise, suspicion towards foreigners. This need for personal time, freedom and challenge is associated with hedonism (pleasure as a reward for freedom). Therefore in high IDV cultures, enjoyment is a strong factor. If the Christian worker cannot enjoy his ministry, he is more likely to be a problem, leave the field or move to find one that is more enjoyable. Collective cultures stress duty and in fact reflect low interpersonal trust with each other, possibly due to conflict over fewer resources and a feeling of having to preserve their status in the society.

In low IDV societies members joining an organisation will transfer their loyalty and allegiance to their culture to the organisation, but will also expect that organisation to respond in the same way. This can be a source of conflict and misunderstanding between low IDV people joining high (western) IDV organisations. The challenge for a multi-national mission is to be able to adapt to the variety of PD and IDV that members will have.

The consequences of individualism on religious life are as follows in Fig 5.8 p. 173 [150] and for an organisation [153].

III Masculinity

Cultures can also be defined as being masculine or feminine. The predominant social pattern is for men to be assertive and women to be nurturing. Businesses have masculine goals and tend to promote men, whilst hospitals are more feminine and nurturing on the nursing side and tend to promote women.

Country	MASC Act-ual	MASC Control-ling for % Women	Country	MASC Act-ual	MASC Control-ling for % Women
A Japan	95	87	C Brazil	49	44
C Austria	79	75	A Singapore	48	52
C Venezuela	73	70	P Israel	47	41
C Italy	70	72	A Turkey	45	53
P Switzerland	70	67	A Taiwan	45	38
C Mexico	69	64	A Iran	43	52
C Ireland	68	74	C France	43	41
P Great Britain	66	66	C Spain	42	35
P Germany (FR)	66	59	C Peru	42	32
	64	58	A Thailand	34	45
C Philippines	64	56	C Portugal	31	32
C Colombia	63	60	C Chile	28	26
P South Africa	62	—a	P Finland	26	51
P USA	61	59	P Denmark	16	22
P Australia	58	55	P Netherlands	14	—b
P New Zealand	57	73	P Norway	8	10
A Greece	57	61	P Sweden	5	6
A Hong Kong	56	50			
A Argentina	56	47			
A India	54	53			
C Belgium	52	53			
P Canada	50	40			
A Pakistan					

C=Catholic, P= Protestant A=Asian

Figure 7: Country Masculinity Index (MASC)

Because of the mothering role of women they tend to be preoccupied with the needs of the family, whilst men have been those concerned with the economy of the family. In giving birth women experience irreversible achievement, whilst men constantly seek that fulfilment in life. The male is always on the search for this same sense of achievement, whether in business, exploration, science or war. This male assertiveness and female nurturing role is common in all nations and all peoples. Gen. 1 would suggest equal partnership in roles but different responsibilities.

In the American Quaker movement it has been found that women are much more self-assured and important in the community, where they have well defined nurturing roles. The community as a whole downplays "What do you do?", a threat to those who have not achieved, and concentrates on "Who are you?"

Ambition can be seen in a positive light in that it is a quest for fulfilment. A contented person may well have less ambition but not less ability. Fear of failure in academic achievement is frequent amongst girls but much rarer with boys during the years of puberty. Men tend to feel threatened by intellectually superior women and want wives who are inferior to them. In many societies this is formalised in the attributes that the matchmaker in a village will look for in matching partners.

The goals of organisations will determine the kind of people they attract. If the emphasis or presentation is upon strategic goals, then men will gravitate to the organisation. With the presentation of suffering the female nurturing instinct comes to the fore and the organisation will attract women. Missions today tend to be oversubscribed 3:1 by women. This may also reflect other factors like men being accepted in pastoral positions and women having to find their Christian service in other areas.

Women have consistently scored higher in tests for interpersonal skills. In fig. 5.1 we have several sets of data: a ranking of Masculine / Feminine by country and an identification of whether that is an Asian (A), Catholic (C) or Protestant (P) country. All the Scandinavian countries score low on the masculine scale. Japan is highest with UK high. The terms M / F refer to learned styles of interpersonal interaction accepted in a given society. They then tend to sustain the dichotomy of the sexes.

Stress is probably the result of leadership. Remember, it is not sex but the sex role that is being identified. Separated or widowed women in Africa have been found to have higher stress levels than married women. Stress could be a factor for the high heart disease in masculine countries. Japan has produced giant corporations and American missions think of size as being important. One American mission set out to be the biggest of its kind and openly boasts that.

Knowing friends and networking has become a mark of modern western missions versus ability. Especially in Muslim missions we are finding leaders emerging based upon networks who have never learned a Muslim language, lived in a Muslim land or even witnessed to a Muslim. Asians will quickly see through this western scenario and reject these modern forms. The corporation concept belongs to the Masculine world and is out of step with Muslim (Feminine) cultures. In Masculine countries people tend to be sceptical of others and rely upon knowing important people and using them. In Feminine cultures people are more loyal, patient of others and servant orientated. In Masculine cultures people 'live to work'; in Feminine ones 'they work to live'.

One study which brought out the Masculine / Feminine traits of a nation was a survey of children's books. In some countries male and female sex roles were shown equally. In Russia and Romania more females were shown and in Sweden both were shown in non-traditional roles such as a boy as a baby-sitter. This fits well with the extreme position of Sweden as a feminine culture.

In some countries there is a show of ostentatious manliness, usually attributed to Latin lands. The female equivalent is marianismo (machismo being the male side), the qualities of which are saintliness, submissiveness and frigidity. This could be related to an undue concentration on the person of the Virgin Mary. Machismo, in fact, is seen to be more prevalent around the Caribbean than in the rest of South America. British working class young people display the same tendency towards machismo.

In Iran men are expected to show their emotions. This comes from the Moharram month of mourning for the 'saints' - Ali and his family - each year. Men read poetry, are sensitive, not expected to be logical, they often embrace, kiss and hold hands with other men. Women are seen to be cold and practical, which was my experience in Iran. The women are far closer culturally to USA men than their menfolk. The sex roles are reversed between USA and Iran.

The Dutch with a low masculine culture have little difference between the sexes psychologically. I shall never forget driving overnight from London to Bolton one year in an old bread van. In it was a mixed team of 8 people. We got a flat tyre but had no jack to lift the van to get the wheel off. A Dutch girl surprised us all by holding it up in order to give time to replace the wheel with the flat tyre quickly, something we Brits would have expected a man to do.

Low MASC	High MASC
• People orientation	• Money and things orientation
• Quality of life and environment are important	• Performance and growth are important
• Work to live	• Live to work
• Service ideal	• Achievement ideal
• Interdependence ideal	• Independence ideal
• Intuition	• Decisiveness
• Sympathy for the unfortunate	• Sympathy for the successful achiever
• Levelling: don't try to be better than others	• Excelling: try to be the best
• Small and slow are beautiful	• Big and fast are beautiful
• Men need to be assertive but can also take caring roles	• Men should behave assertively and women should care
• Sex roles in society should be fluid	• Sex roles in society should be clearly differentiated
• Differences in sex roles should not mean differences in power	• Men should dominate in all settings
• Unisex and androgyny ideal	• Machismo (ostentative manliness) ideal

Figure 8: The Masculinity Societal Norm

Countries closer to the equator tend to be more masculine, towards the poles more feminine. In PD there is a logical relationship between latitude and milder climates. Cold climates produce the need for heating and survival, producing technology and wealth leading to greater co-operation, thus low PD and high IDV. Also in mild climates survival presupposes the mastery of complex skills by women and men, thus reducing inequality between the sexes.

The message of the OT seems to be more masculine and that of the NT feminine. Thus Christians find support for what they hold to by appealing to whichever form they choose: the OT with its law "an eye for an eye" and the NT with its "turning the other cheek".

Catholicism has produced some very masculine societies, such as the Templars and Jesuits, but also the Franciscans, who care for the poor. Protestantism likewise has produced masculine movements like Mormons and fundamentalist sects, but generally Catholicism produces masculine cultures and Protestantism feminine ones. Protestant churches have always had a role for women and even more so today, whilst Catholicism has always been led by men.

We can see from fig. 6 that Scandinavian levels are high in feminine traits (low in masculinity). A possible reason for this is the need to survive in a harsh climate. The men supplemented their food stocks by raiding down the North Sea and the English Channel, leaving the women at home to run affairs.

IV Uncertainty Avoidance

Uncertainty in life is a basic fact that all of us experience - how we deal with those uncertainties will largely depend on our culture. These are reflected in technology, rules and ritual. We live in the tension of past and future, how to live in the present is a question we all respond to consciously or unconsciously. Some retreat into the past for sure guidelines as Islamic fundamentalists do - looking at the life of Muhammad as a source for certain behaviour. No creative thinking is needed or wanted. It is always easier to live under law than grace. Grace produces uncertainty, law certainty. Nazism was an escape from the uncertainty of being free. This ever-present uncertainty of life produces a means to deal with it in all human artefacts, law both formal and informal, which guide behaviour, and religion, which is a revelation of the unknown. Many of the ways of dealing with life do not in fact create certainty, but they allow us to rest hoping they will. Fig. 8 shows Germany with a low tolerance (the lowest of all Protestant countries) to uncertainty and thus Nazism was a response to those pressures of unemployment etc. that came after the first world war. It was a security to know that a strong man was in charge. Totalitarian organisations try to avoid uncertainty.

Today our environment is changing rapidly; weather, communications, work, family, sexuality seemed to have changed rapidly in the last 10 years. This has given rise to a number of authoritarian sects around the world offering refuge from such a world - or at least an interpretation of it. When changes take place, members of

UAI		UAI	
Country		**Country**	
1.	Greece	21.	Thailand
2.	Portugal	22.	Iran
3.	Belgium	23.	Finland
4.	Japan	24.	Switzerland
5.	Peru	25.	Netherlands
6.	France	26.	Australia
7.	Chile	27.	Norway
8.	Spain	28.	South Africa
9.	Argentina	29.	New Zealand
10.	Turkey	30.	Canada
11.	Mexico	31.	USA
12.	Israel	32.	Philippines
13.	Colombia	33.	India
14.	Venezuela	34.	Great Britain
15.	Brazil	35.	Ireland
16.	Italy	36.	Hong Kong
17.	Pakistan	37.	Sweden
18.	Austria	38.	Denmark
19.	Taiwan	39.	Singapore
20.	Germany (FR)		

Figure 9: Country Uncertainty Avoidance Index (UAI)

an organisation may rebel and seek to replace the leadership if it does not provide security and protection from the storm.

Organisations avoid uncertainty either by focusing on short-run reaction to pressuring problems and not anticipating longer term issues or by setting up standard operating procedures and avoiding planning; it becomes the science of muddling through.

Low UAI Countries	High UAI Countries
• Lower anxiety level in population	· Higher anxiety level in population
• Greater readiness to live by the day	· More worry about the future
• Lower job stress	· Higher job stress
• Less emotional resistance to change	• More emotional resistance to change
• Less hesitation to change employers	• Tendency to stay with the same employer
• Loyalty to employers is not seen as a virtue	• Loyalty to employers is seen as a virtue
• Preference for smaller organisations as employers	• Preference for larger organisations as employers
• Smaller generation gap	• Greater generation gap
• Lower average age in higher level jobs	• Higher average age in higher level jobs: gerontocracy
• Managers should be selected on other criteria than seniority	• Managers should be selected on the basis of seniority
• Stronger achievement motivation	• Less achievement motivation
• Hope of success	• Fear of failure
• More risk taking	• Less risk-taking
• Stronger ambition for individual advancement	• Lower ambition for individual advancement
• Prefers manager career over specialist career	• Prefers specialist career to manager career
• A manager need not be an expert in the field he manages	• A manager must be an expert in the field he manages
• Hierarchical structures of organisations can be bypassed for pragmatic reasons.	• Hierarchical structures of organisations should be clear and respected
• Preference for broad guidelines	• Preference for clear requirements and instructions
• Rules may be broken for pragmatic reasons	• Company rules should not be broken

Low UAI Countries	High UAI Countries
• Conflict in organisations is natural	• Conflict in organisations is undesirable
• Competition between employees can be fair and right	• Competition between employees is emotionally disapproved of
• More sympathy for individual and authoritative decisions	• Ideological appeal of consensus and of consultative leadership
• Delegation to subordinates can be complete	• However, initiative of subordinates should be kept under control
• Higher tolerance for ambiguity in perceiving others (higher LPC)	• Lower tolerance for ambiguity in perceiving others (lower LPC)
• More prepared to compromise with opponents	• Lower readiness to compromise with opponents
• Acceptance of foreigners as managers	• Suspicion toward foreigners as managers
• Larger fraction prepared to live abroad	• Fewer people prepared to live abroad
• Higher tolerance for ambiguity in looking at own job (lower satisfaction scores)	• Lower tolerance for ambiguity in looking at own job (higher satisfaction scores)
• Citizen optimism about ability to control politicians' decisions	• Citizen pessimism about ability to control politicians' decisions
• Employee optimism about the motives behind company activities	• Employee pessimism about the motives behind company activities
• Optimism about people's amount of initiative, ambition, and leadership skills	• Pessimism about people's amount of initiative, ambition, and leadership skills.

Figure 10: **A Summary of Connotations of Uncertainty Avoidance Index Differences**

Figure 11: **A Summary of Implications of Uncertainty Avoidance Index Differences.**

Internal uncertainty can be dealt with by setting up rules that deal with a specific issue from the past so that it never happens again. Bureaucracy is the response to uncertainty. In some ways these rules are irrational, because they try to make people predictable. A mission with a large and growing procedures manual is the result of unsure people not wanting to trust its members to act and be loyal in the interests of the Lord or the church. Good rules can set people free to create and need not be constraining; bad rules arise out of people making them being out of touch with those who have to follow them. Bad rules can remove a person's sense of judgement, just as with soldiers who have to obey officers and who are ordered to torture someone: "an order is an order".

Planning is the fertility rite of business. Cavemen drew pictures of the animals they were to kill. No one, however, can anticipate the future - we can only look back. Random trial and error is more likely to produce results than planning. I remember feeling the need to challenge the Orthodox churches in Russia to get involved in Muslim mission and I produced a book in Russian towards that end. My team felt I was mad and unbusiness-like, but the same year was the millennium celebration and all went very well. Planning, given the current conditions, dictated caution, but trial and error produced fruit. It shook those around me who needed the security of "knowing" their perception of a secure future and was to reap bitter consequences in the years to come in rebellion.

Another method of facing uncertainty is to appoint experts. They are the sorcerers of primitive society. These experts do not really know but they give a "feel good" factor to those using them. What expert fund-raiser lives on a percentage of what he raises? They all want their fee up front irrespective of whether they are successful.

Employment contracts and rule orientation are two ways to avoid uncertainty. Uncertainty produces stress and some cannot live like that. Stress is not bad of itself. Unrelieved stress can destroy and break a person and so we need to vary our work patterns, pace of life and interests. Hard work never killed anyone; constant stress can. I like to think I work hard - it is a thing I enjoy, but I also have varied interests like writing, fishing, gardening, fixing my car, breeding fish, etc, etc. Stress also prepares us for aggression and when society forbids this aggression it finds other ways to cope. Sri Lanka was known as an island of tranquillity with a gentle people, as are Thailand and SE Asia, but witness the incredible cruelty in the wars there; the cork blew out and men reverted to being men.

Excess stress has been shown to produce heart disease risk, stomach disorders, nervous breakdown and reduced intellectual ability. Higher stress goes with a strong rule orientation and greater employment stability and vice versa. Figure 8 shows how nations score on the uncertainty list. Many Asian countries come lower in the scale, but not as low as Protestant countries.

High uncertainty avoidance has the following characteristics:

- Low ambition for advancement, a preference for specialist rather than management position.

- Preference for large organisations and approval for loyalty.

- A tendency to avoid competition amongst employees.

- Dislike of working for a foreigner.

- Resistance to change.

- A pessimistic outlook on the motives of the company.

- The level of satisfaction depends on the lack of uncertainty.

Latinos with a high anxiety level prevent illness by being expressive and talkative. A low UA means a greater willingness to take risks. Can you imagine the problem in an organisation where the leader has a low anxiety level and takes risks and his accounts department or deputy has a high UA? One day he will gain enough support from others to risk being disloyal and ousting the leader, which often happens, and then settles down to a quiet life, thus losing the inspiration that gave the organisation its drive and vision. Death ensues.

UA is also seen to be dependent upon age. In a high UA older people wait longer before handing over to the next generation - just to be sure about their capabilities - maybe old people rule for longer in these societies. They also like group decisions as a way of avoiding risk. Because of these cultural characteristics it can naturally be seen that a leader may be effective in one country but totally ineffective in a different environment.

In reverse I have seen people who appear to be 'odd' and misfits in church life in the UK actually blossom and be successful in an Asian context. Some of this may be due to the docility of Asians to westerners or to respect for an older or educated person, but it has also been because they "jibe" or empathise more easily with the host culture. The removal from a success driven culture may also allow them to relax and perform better. People in low UA

countries believe they can help to bring about peace and that compromise is not dangerous. They are prepared to live one day at a
time and are willing to live abroad. This makes them excellent
potential missionaries.

Just as those nations with a cultural inheritance from the Roman Empire had high PD scores, so also they have a high UA.
Legislation helps to predict the future and control events. In its turn
it reinforces that norm. Germany has extensive laws even for events
that have not yet occurred. Great Britain does not even have a
written constitution and attempts to codify labour-management relations failed because they were against the norms of that society.
One of the ways by which the Roman Empire perpetuates itself is
through legislation.

In low UA countries like Denmark, Sweden and the UK there
is no obligation to carry ID cards; people are content not to have
to identify themselves to policemen.

IN high UA lands ID cards are strictly enforced, this is where
the citizen must prove himself before the authorities, whereas in
low UA the state has the burden of proof.

Religion is one way of dealing with the unknown. High UA
countries have religions that stress absolute certainties (abortion,
papal infallibility, Sharia law) and are intolerant of other religions
(inquisition, Islamic apostasy). As western education with its critical approach to all areas of life permeates the world via education,
TV, film and literature, there is a growing backlash born out of a
need to avoid uncertainty in Muslim lands. This is expressed in
oppression of minorities (Pakistan, Sudan, Egypt, Iran), calls for the
death penalty for critics of Islam (they are enemies of God) and
accusations of blasphemy against other religions (Gul Masih).
Interestingly enough, Buddhism is not concerned with absolutes
and in Buddhist lands we find low UA; Chinese people have been
seen to have a relativistic approach to morality. High UA countries
look at problems ideologically but low UA sees them in a pragmatic
light.

In games these forces can be seen at work. Games fall into 3
types.

1) Games of physical skill where mastery of self and the environment are required. (Technology).

2) Games of strategy which aim to master the social system. (Law).

3) Games of chance which aim at mastery of the supernatural. (Religion).

In high UA areas scholars look for certainties in theory and truth; in low UA they have a pragmatic approach to life and look for usable knowledge. Most Nobel peace prize recipients come from low UA. The great philosophers and theoreticians come from high UA areas like Germany and Austria: Kant, Marx, Freud, Weber and Popper.

These countries do not produce empirical studies in the social studies area, whereas Great Britain and the USA are full of them. Recognising and accepting these predilections is important for the overall functioning of the body of Christ, as each culture plays its part in the whole.

An attempt to create a United States of Europe is fraught with difficulties and the arguments over roads to take contrast with one another. France and Germany seem to see the possibility, in theory, of a total merger based upon a common currency. The UK holds out for a more pragmatic loose alliance of states. To submerge cultural differences as varied as exist in Europe from Greece to Denmark could be asking for major conflicts and a backlash from the peoples of the lands. The high UA theoreticism needs to accept the low UA pragmatist approach and vice versa and get married.

The UA norm deals with a level of anxiety about future events in a country or organisation. A higher anxiety leads to stress and a hurried social life. On a high UA aggressiveness and the showing of emotions are seen and these societies created the means to express them in talkativeness, hand and body movements; low UA countries do not approve of an outward show of emotion, the British reserve is well known and the butt of many jokes by Americans etc.

People in high UA look for consensus in decision making. A team made up of predominantly high UA members but led by a low

UA may well have conflicts and possible rebellion against the leader if he does not follow their group decision making. However this high UA group is less tolerant of people of other ideas and behaviour patterns. Change in high UA is resisted; law and order is a priority.

Organisations of high UA will be uniform, such as Open Doors, which could be seen to be higher than the national norm; lower UA ones will be very diverse, like OM.

German and French managers need to be better informed in order to keep an eye on details, a sure sign of UA. British managers look to strategy more. I remember an Iranian team member complaining of me that I only thought about projects and strategy in the work in Iran. He was interested in feelings and needing a warm atmosphere. To my mind a warm woolly atmosphere does not reach the masses, but a good strategy makes it happen - a classic case of culture conflict.

A leader gives hope, a vision of the future that those with high UA can trust and fall in behind, but if he fails they will cry "crucify him" once again.

These four categories PD / IDV / Masc/ UA are universal categories of culture. They deal with:

- Relationship to Authority in PD.
- Conception of self i.e. - Masculinity, Individualism.
- Dilemmas and conflict and how to deal with them - UA.

In the high PD, high UA areas all Latin, Mediterranean countries plus Japan appear. The strong super ego will be personified in a powerful person in law, government, church, sect and leader arena. They will blame other people for their ills and sin, if no one is looking.

Other Asian countries are found in high PD low UA or medium UA.

In low PD high UA we have German speakers plus Israel and Finland. Here super ego is internalised and we find Freud being Austrian. Low PD low UA are Anglo-Scandinavian lands, which have greater experimentation with alternative behaviour. In UK everything is permitted except what is forbidden. In Germany everything is forbidden except what is permitted. In France everything is permitted - even that which is forbidden.

In cultures where there is high PD power is the leading principle which keeps the organisation together, like the Pope. In low PD organisations there are two options. If people have a need for values which reflect a high UA, formal rules governing behaviour need to be verbalised. If not, then ad hoc negotiation is possible. I was thrown out of an organisation I founded because the office staff of high UA needed formal rules to guide them and I was used to leading by ad hoc negotiation; the tension for them was explosive. Normally Matt. 18, if brought into play, would have resolved those issues and, if the qualities of loyalty, love and patience had been applied, then these tensions could have been discussed, but the split was no different from one in any secular London firm. My leadership skills were sadly lacking to deal with this complexity of forces.

The French have been seen to resolve their problems by referring to the hierarchy, the British by horizontal negotiation, the Germans by procedures. Asians tend to function in family units and therefore a personal bureaucracy emerges, relationship being determined by a hierarchical framework.

Time is a factor of culture. For the Germans it is a source of pressure; they are constantly aware of its passing. For the French it is a resource to be controlled and utilised, for the British it is a tool for orientating oneself. Therefore there is no one best way but a variety of approaches which the cultural norms will select as being relevant and the right leader will make work effectively in any given environment.

Latin Americans focus on power (power evangelism came out of LA), Central Europe and Germany on truth (Bultmann, Bonhoffer, Kirkegaard), Eastern Europe on efficiency, Northern Europe on change and in Western Europe the Dutch and British concentrate on data collection (Johnston, Operation World; Barrett, Encyclopaedia of Christianity; Brierley, UK Christian Handbook. All Britishers).

Only by comparing cultures shall we find that other ideas are possible. Water will be the last thing a fish discovers when he is landed. Only out of our culture shall we understand just how all-pervasive our culture is in our thinking. Missions - short-term and longer term - have the possibility of changing us permanently. Our ideas are so tangled up in our values and interests which we recognise in others but not in ourselves.

In matching workers for the Muslim world we have had to identify the cultural linguistic blocs of Islam. These fall into 5 basic blocs: Arab, Turk, Malay, Indo-Persian, African (Nilotic, Chad). We have assumed that the language is the carrier of the culture for all interests and purposes.

Koreans find English hard to learn but feel at home in Turkey, being both linguistically able to learn Turkish faster than English and also recognising cultural similarities, e.g. Shamanistic practices, monocultural, monolinguistic thinking, militarism.

Filipinos relate well to Malays and settle in quickly. I met a team from Solomon Islands in Singapore who felt at home and could relate well to Malays. This should be, since Malayo-Polynesian languages are spoken on all the Pacific islands.

Summary. With the injection of large numbers of Anglo-Saxon missionaries from Asia, Africa and Latin America we are having to re-evaluate just what contribution has been made to missions. Both seem to have positive cultural insights into the task ahead and therefore all must take time to listen, understand and integrate approaches to world evangelism. Given the strengths of each culture, there must be a greater willingness to share resources in manpower, finances and learning, *without strings attached* but with a willingness to share, give account and consider one another's positions. Given the economic climate, much more consideration must be given to wealth creation, trading, funding and resourcing of those who are in a better position to reach the Muslim cultures. New methods of education must be developed. Western education does not fit an Asian to relate to his people. Mentoring seems to be much more appropriate.

Overall the future looks bright, if we can learn from one another. There will be tensions, but a commitment to loyalty will overrule these pressures. Without it we shall break up.

Culture is to play a major role in church planting; can we not let those who intuitively relate to the target culture do the work ?

Ron George
WIN International Associates
Crowborough
England.

APPENDIX B
Resources

The following three sections provide suggested resources for further reading or use on:

1) various aspects of Islam,

2) your development as a cross-cultural worker with Muslims, and

3) materials for use with your Muslim friends.

ISLAMICS
Muhammad:

Andrae, Tor. 1956 Mohammed, the Man and His Faith, Translated from the German. London: George Allen and Unwin Ltd.
A serious but very readable study based on knowledge and immense research, which avoids extremes in interpreting the life of Muhammad.

Cragg, Kenneth. 1984 Muhammad and the Christian: A Question of Response, DLT and Orbis.
How are Christians to answer Muslims who genuinely want to know how we think about Muhammad?

Watt, W. Montgomery. 1961 Muhammad - Prophet and Statesman. London: Oxford University Press.
A series of detailed, classical studies by an outstanding scholar.

THE HOLY BOOK OF ISLAM-THE QUR'AN
Ali, Abdullah Yusuf. 1938 The Meaning of the Glorious Quran. Vol. I - II, Dar Al-Kitab Al-Masri, Egypt.
Arabic text and English translations of the Qur'an with extensive commentary.

Cragg, Kenneth. 1971 The Event of the Qur'an. Islam in its Scripture. London: George Allen and Unwin Ltd. *A modern Christian attempt sympathetically, yet critically, to assess the meaning and significance of the Qur'an as an "event"*

*- not simply a document - fusing Muhammad's personal charisma, poetic elo-
quence, Arab consciousness and vibrant theism into the Scripture of Islam.*

Maududi, S. Abul A'la. 1976 The meaning of the Quran. Vol. I - VIII. Lahore,
Pakistan: Pan Islamic Publishers, 13-E, Shahalam Market.
*A commentary on the Qur'an written by a leading Pakistani reformer and
scholar.*

Parrinder, Geoffrey. 1965 Jesus in the Qur'an. London: Faber and Faber.
*A book intended for both Christians and Muslims. The author systematically
collects Qur'anic teachings about Jesus and His associates and discusses them
in the light of parallels in the Bible.*

Watt, W. Montgomery. 1967 Companion to the Qur'an. London: George Allen
and Unwin Ltd.
*Notes on the Qur'anic text giving helpful background information and explain-
ing allusions which western readers might not understand. Based on Arberry's
translation, but can be used with any translation. Contains a useful index of
proper names in the Qur'an.*

MUSLIM BELIEFS AND PRACTICES

Cragg, Kenneth. 1969 House of Islam. Dickenson, California.
*Wonderful exposition by England's leading Islamicist on the five articles of
Muslim belief.*

Fellowship of Faith for Muslims n.d. "Focus on Islam" booklets. York, England.
*A series of inexpensive, informative booklets which may be useful in introduc-
ing laypeople to the nature and challenges of Islam. Titles include:*

• "The Muslim Challenge to the Christian Church",
• "Islam: What is It?",
• "The Five Pillars of Islam",
• "The Ahmadiyya Movement",
• "The Life of Muslim Women",
• "From Islam to Christ - How a Sufi Found his Lord",
• and "The Qur'an Says..."

Rahman, Fazlur. 1979 Islam. Second Edition. Chicago: University of Chicago
Press.
*A descriptive and interpretative explanation of Islam and of the general history
of ideas in the Muslim world by a key Muslim spokesman.*

von Grunebaum, G. E. 1951 Muhammadan Festivals. New York: Henry
Schuman.
*The story of the main Muhammadan festivals from their origins to the present
day.*

Hussein, Kamel. 1995 City of Wrong: A Friday in Jerusalem.
*A thoughtful Muslim reflects on the crucifixion. Translated by Kenneth
Cragg.*

THE DEVELOPMENT OF ISLAMIC CULTURES

Beck, Lois and Nikki Keddi, (Eds). 1978 Women in the Muslim World. Cambridge: Harvard University Press.
*Contains 33 original essays written by experts who have lived and studied in
main parts of the Muslim world covering historical and contemporary roles of
Muslim women in nomadic, rural and urban Islamic societies and the influence
of ideology, religion and ritual upon their lives.*

Fernea, Elizabeth Warnock and Basima Qattan Bezirgan. 1978 Middle Eastern
Muslim Women Speak. Austin: University of Texas Press.
*Collection of autobiographical and biographical writings by and about Middle
Eastern women representative of a wide range of occupations, perspectives
and socio-economic status as well as views on major issues concerning women
in the contemporary Muslim world.*

Levy, Reuben. 1957 The Social Structure of Islam. London: Cambridge University Press.
*A sociological study of the effects which the religious system of Islam has on
Muslim communities, noting the common features of their social structure
with respect to social classes, the status of women and children, morality, law,
etc.*

Mernissi, Fatima. 1975 Beyond the Veil. Schenkman Pub. Comp., Mass.
*A detailed analysis of female/male dynamics in a modern Muslim Society,
invaluable insights.*

Patai, Raphael. 1976 The Arab Mind. New York: Charles Scribner's Sons.
*Study of the Arab society, its traditions and way of life and its effects on
contemporary Middle Eastern problems.*

Lewis, Philip. 1994 Islamic Britain: Religion, Politics and identity among British
Muslims. Bradford in the 1990's. I.B. Tauris.
*A detailed study of this Muslim community. It provides a model for living
among Muslims.*

PRESENT DAY TENSIONS IN ISLAM

Cragg, Kenneth. 1965 Counsels in Contemporary Islam. (Islamic Surveys Series, No. 3) Edinburgh University Press.
*A survey of the main currents of Islamic reaction to the modern world in the
Arab East, Turkey, Pakistan and India.*

Smith, Wilfred Cantwell. 1957 Islam in Modern History. Princetown University Press.
A basically sympathetic, yet keenly critical, view beneath the surface of events, providing perceptive insight into the tension between faith and history in the Muslim world.

Pullapilly, Cyriac (Ed). 1980 Islam in the Contemporary World. Cross Roads Books.
A collection of extremely good essays on Islam today.

Esposito, John. 1992 The Islamic Threat: Myth or Reality? Oxford University Press.
An excellent survey, challenging popular western conceptions of Islam. Gives background to the Iranian, Sudanese and Algerian problems.

FOR THE CHRISTIAN WORKER

Books:

Abdul-Haqq, Abdiyah Akbar. 1980 Sharing Your Faith with a Muslim. Minneapolis: Bethany Fellowship, Inc.
The person of Christ, the key biblical concepts of sin, salvation and the nature of God beautifully articulated from the point of view of communicating them to a Muslim inquirer.

Christensen, Jens. 1977 The Practical Approach to Muslims. North Africa Mission.
A timely reprint of a stimulating study course first published serially in Pakistan by a Lutheran bishop who spent a lifetime working among Muslim Pathans on the Northwest Frontier. Bishop Christensen was an original thinker who held that the basic problem in the mission to Islam is theological and he calls for an honest rethinking of our approach to Islam which is both radical and practical.

Cragg, Kenneth. 1964 The Call of the Minaret. London: Oxford University Press.
The first and perhaps the best of Dr. Cragg's many books. A penetrating and stimulating interpretation of Islam based on the phrases of the call to prayer as given five times a day by the muezzin. He first analyses what the call to prayer means to the Muslim, historically and doctrinally. Then he finds in it, for the Christian, a call to understanding, to service, to retrieval, to interpretation and to patience.

Dretke, James P. 1979 A Christian Approach to Muslims. Reflections from West Africa. Pasadena: William Carey Library.
Basic questions and answers common to Muslim/Christian interaction on many different aspects of faith presented in a conversational format between author and West African Muslims.

Elder, John. 1974 Biblical Approach to the Muslims. Fort Washington: World-wide Evangelization Crusade.
Brief coverage of history of Islam followed by analysis of Islam and Christianity as basis of an apologetic approach. Each chapter is followed by questions for review.

Fellowship of Faith for Muslims. 1976 Your Muslim Guest, A Practical Guide in Friendship and Witness for Christians Who Meet Muslims in North America. Toronto: Fellowship of Faith for Muslims.
The purpose of this 15-page booklet is clear from the subtitle. It is especially helpful for people meeting and entertaining Muslim guests for the first time.

Friends of Turkey; A Witness Handbook for Persons Living or Working Among Turks. Available from: Friends of Turkey, 277 Oak., Grand Junction, CO 81503.
An excellent beginning in helping you become equipped for working with Turkish people. Presents some cultural cues and pointers in sharing the Christian faith.

Goldsmith, Martin. 1982 Islam and Christian Witness. Hodder & Stoughton, London.
One of the best books to start with for an understanding of Islam and being an effective witness.

Lenning, Larry G. 1980 Blessing in Mosque and Mission. Pasadena: William Carey Library.
A well-researched effort aimed at building constructive bridges to African Muslims through the dynamic concept of blessing. It includes extensive documentation of Islamic and biblical material which presents the Christian worker with numerous avenues for meeting Muslims with the gospel.

Marsh, Charles R. 1975 Share Your Faith with a Muslim. Chicago: Moody Press.
A practical little book by a veteran missionary in North America on "do's and don'ts" of working with Muslim men and women. Shows great insight into issues between Muslims and Christians.

McCurry, Don M., (Ed). 1978 The Gospel and Islam: a 1978 Compendium. Monrovia: Missions Advanced Research and Communication Centre.
Forty study papers and conference reports present the key issues being faced in Muslim evangelism today and an overview of the extent of Islam worldwide; and also current thinking on new approaches in Muslim evangelism. A key text for Christian workers.

Musk, Bill A. 1995 Touching the Soul of Islam. Marc Monarch Publications.
Explores the Islamic world view in order to communicate with and understand Muslim people.

Nehls, Gerhard. 1980 Christians Ask Muslims. Christians Answer Muslims. Life Challenge, South Africa.
Two excellent books on basic information.

Parshall, Philip. 1980 New Paths in Muslim Evangelism. Grand Rapids: Baker Book House.
This book deals with the efforts to disciple Muslims of Bangladesh who have come to Christ and who are designing their own form and structure of fellowships from the Bible alone in a Muslim context.

Spencer, H. 1967 Islam and the Gospel of God. Delhi: S.P.C.K.
A Comparison of the central doctrines of Christianity and Islam prepared as a useful tool for Christian workers, translators and writers among Muslims. Recently reprinted because of renewed demand.

Vander Werff, Lyle L. 1977 Christian Mission to Muslims. The Record, Anglican and Reformed Approaches in India and the Near East, 1800-1938. Pasadena: William Carey Library.
A doctrinal study analysing lessons learned in the mission to Muslims from the time of Henry Martyn to Samuel Zwemer.

Wilson, J. Christy Today's Tentmakers. Self-support: An alternative model for world-wide witness. Wheaton, Il: Tyndale House Publishers, Inc.
A handbook for prospective tentmakers, including information on foreign travel and employment, support organisations, language training, moving, cultural adjustment and politics. Excellent bibliography and list of organisations with addresses on all aspects of tentmaking.

Films:

Islam: Unlocking the Door. 1981 Produced by World Vision International. Directed by James Greenelsh. 35 minutes, 16mm.
A documentary highlighting issues and attitudes germane to understanding Islam and developing more sensitive approaches to Muslim peoples.

FOR MUSLIMS
Books:

Accad, Fuad E. 197- Have You Ever Read the Seven Muslim/Christian Principles? Second edition. Colorado Springs: Navigators.
A contextualised version of the "Four Spiritual Laws" for Muslims, using references from the Bible and the Qur'an in a comparative text format.

Clark, Dennis E. 1977 The Life and Teaching of Jesus the Messiah (Sirat-ul-Masih, Isa, Ibn Maryam). Elgin: Dove Publications.
A carefully prepared life of Christ based on the text of the Gospels, written with Muslim readers in mind by one with much experience in living and working among them. In addition to English, it is available in Arabic and several other languages of the Muslim world.

Fellowship of Isa. 1980 Isa (Jesus Christ) in the Qur'an and the Bible. Minneapolis: Fellowship of Isa.
Short pamphlet outlining:
1) *Qur'anic references about Christ's second coming,*
2) *listing of comparative references from the Qur'an and Injil (Bible) about Christ and*
3) *a brief summary of the gospel message for salvation.*

Finlay, M.H. 1968 Face the Facts, Questions and Answers Concerning the Christian Faith. Bombay: Gospel Literature Service.
Originally written in Singapore, this little manual is just what the subtitle implies. It specifically replies to common Muslim questions about the Bible: the person of Christ and the Trinity.

Hannah, Mark. 1975 The True Path. Seven Muslims Make Their Greatest Discovery. Colorado Springs: The International Doorways Publications.
Testimonies by representative Muslims who have discovered Christ in a personal way. The book concludes with an extensive glossary of Christian terms and appendices presenting additional information about the Bible.

Miller, William M. 1972 Beliefs and Practices of Christians (A Letter to a Friend). Lahore, Pakistan: Mashihi Isha'at Khana.
An excellent brief guide to Christian beliefs, well written for Muslims in terms and categories which they understand.

Wootton, R.W.F. 1982 Jesus More than a Prophet. I.V.P. London.
15 Muslims tell how they came to Christ as Saviour.